# Fabulous Furniture Decorations

*Books by Leslie Linsley*

Decoupage, A New Look At an Old Craft
Decoupage Designs
Scrimshaw
The Decoupage Workshop
Decoupage for Young Crafters
Wildcrafts
Decoupage On
Air Crafts
Fabulous Furniture Decorations

# Fabulous Furniture Decorations

by Leslie Linsley

photographs by Jon Aron

Thomas Y. Crowell Company, New York Established 1834

## acknowledgments

When creating an instructive craft book the first stage is determining what the projects will be. Next is designing those projects and finally gathering the exact materials needed to execute the ideas. I am most appreciative for the help I received in efficiently obtaining the materials needed to present the projects as planned. I would like to thank Betsey Brooks and Pat Pinkerton at J. C. Penney Co.; Audrey Pierce, Ana Lopo and Phyliss Melhado at 3M; Nina Klippel for the Borden's company; Bob Moss of The Wood Shed, Westport, Conn.; Arthur Brown; Sam Flacks of The Wood Panel Center, Westport, Conn.; Philan Distributors; and Philip and Camille for a great place to work.

FIRST EDITION

*Designed by Jon Aron*

**Library of Congress Cataloging in Publication Data**

Linsley, Leslie.
    Fabulous Furniture Decorations.
    1. Furniture finishing. I. Title.
TT199.4.L56 1978      684.1′043      77–13106
ISBN 0–690–01698–0

78 79 80 81 82 10 9 8 7 6 5 4 3 2 1

# contents

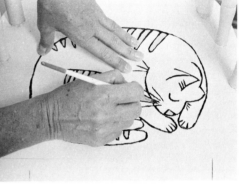

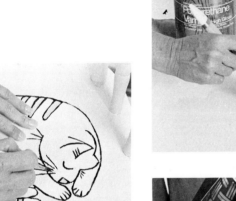

# Fabulous Furniture Decorations

# why unfinished furniture?

Over the years the price of furniture, as most of you know, has skyrocketed. It is almost impossible for a young couple to furnish an apartment when they first move in. And as families expand, extra pieces of furniture are usually needed. A few years ago there was a spurt of books aimed at helping to solve these problems by telling us how to make our own furniture. For families on the move as jobs changed, these books gave instructions for making fold-up, knock-down, easy-to-move furniture, which became a new craze for a while. I read the books and envied all the people who were actually following their lead. But I didn't want to make my own furniture. I get impatient, even with easy-to-follow directions. My talents in carpentry extend as far as hammering a nail or using a screw driver—period. But I also like my environment to be distinctive. I want to live in a home that expresses my personality. I am not an artist, but I consider myself creative, and, without devoting too much effort, I want this to show in the space I occupy for living and working. Unfinished furniture is a perfect solution.

Unfinished, unpainted, ready-to-finish, in-the-raw, whatever you call it, this type of furniture is usually inexpensive and must be sanded, painted, stained or finished in some way before using. It has been available in all parts of the country for years and years. Almost everyone has painted or stained a parson's table or dresser at one time or another. Magazines have often included a painted piece as part of a room setting, and if you look carefully you will find it. But, never before has this ready-to-finish furniture actually been given star billing —put on stage—to be admired for all its virtues.

It is functional and inexpensive when compared to other furniture and it offers creative potential for almost any kind of crafting. Lately, unfinished furniture has been seen regularly on the craft pages of several popular magazines, and retail outlets for buying the various pieces are springing up all over the country. Not only can the furniture be obtained locally but, for those of us living far from large cities, catalog sales are flourishing. While the mail-order furniture is not always delivered completely assembled, the pieces are easy to put together for even the most inexperienced. With the increasing popularity of this kind of furniture, manufacturers have been developing expanded lines and there is almost no item that can't be found.

Among the most widely purchased pieces are parson's tables in varying sizes, from a small 18-inch square up to a full dining table size. They come narrow, short, wide, tall, and often the seller will customize a piece to fit a particular need.

Cubes probably run second to the tables and are most versatile. They are used as storage units, tables, topped with a pillow for occasional seating, grouped together for larger sitting or table space and are easy to move from one room to another as needed. I had the most fun designing this item since almost any idea can be executed with little time, effort and money.

And then came bureaus. For a while I thought I would be doing an entire book on dressers. They have to be the best buy in town. The first project I ever did on unfinished furniture was a decoupaged three-drawer dresser for *Glamour* magazine. I fell in love with it and was absolutely hooked. There was never a more satisfying project because the results are great no matter what you do to the piece. There you are faced with this rather crude, pine dresser and it can only get better. There is absolutely nothing that you can do to that dresser that will make it look worse. Even if you simply paint or stain it, the results are overwhelming. Well, after that first experience I wanted to transform a dresser for everyone in the house, and I did. These bureaus needn't be limited to the bedroom either. A small bureau is handy in a kitchen, dining area, family room or hallway. I find the small size a great advantage because the bureau is not too cumbersome to fit almost anywhere comfortably.

When I began working on this book I ran into a friend. "Unfinished furniture!" she exclaimed. "What a great idea. But I wouldn't even know where to begin. Will it be for people who want to learn refinishing so that the furniture will look like fine furniture pieces?" I assured her that even she would be able to decorate a piece of furniture and that we would not be pretending that the furniture was something it wasn't. We aren't trying to remake the furniture by adding fancy molding or fake finishes. This furniture has to be recognized for what it is. And it is terrific. It is fabulous. Where can you possibly buy a five-drawer dresser for fifty dollars? Sometimes it may need sanding, a spot of glue here and there, even a nail or two for reinforcement. But don't lose sight of the fact that most unfinished furniture is just that: unfinished. You are paying less because you are willing to finish it yourself. Beyond the price, there are many other advantages. Because the furniture is lightweight, you can walk into a store, have the piece loaded into your car within five minutes, and place it in your home that same day. Try doing that in a fine furniture store. With no hitches and a bit of luck the piece of furniture will arrive in six weeks.

Not all unfinished furniture is made in the same way, and some pieces are much better made than others. There are many manufacturers, and each factory has different standards. For better quality furniture you will have to pay more, but you may then need to put less of yourself into preparing it. Some of it is so beautiful that it can be lightly sanded, coated with varnish or rubbed with linseed oil and stand on its own. Often the least expensive furniture must be given more attention in order to make it more durable. So when you begin to look for your own pieces it's a good idea to keep in mind that all unfinished furniture is not alike. Shop around and become knowledgeable. Open drawers and cabinet doors to see how they fit. But, of course, keep in mind that you get what you pay for, so if price is the most important factor don't get angry when you have to fill in a knot hole or sand drawers so that they fit properly. A realistic perspective is necessary.

While obtaining furniture to work on for the book I interviewed a man whose tables turned out to be the best I could find in the area. Arthur Brown has a factory in Danbury, Connecticut, and his parson's tables are sold in many retail stores across the country. It was early spring when we visited Mr. Brown, and we found him bent over his work area. He took Jon and me on a tour of a huge two story building that had the delicious smell of freshly cut wood. We passed rows of tables in the process of being glued. "Quality, tell them to look for quality," he answered when I asked what our readers should look for when buying a piece of unfinished furniture. "I never ship anything that isn't perfect," he continued. He lifted a parson's table to show us a flaw. "Can't send this out," he stated. We looked, but couldn't see a thing wrong with the table. Apparently there was a defect in the wood. "I try to keep my line limited," he added. "If you spread yourself too thin, keep designing new pieces, you can't take the time to perfect what you've got. I stick to the few pieces we made originally and that's all I sell. When you buy an Arthur Brown table, it's made well, it's sturdy and you get your money's worth."

I imagine that many manufacturers feel the same way

about their products. So I pass along the advice. Look a piece over carefully. Check underneath to see how it is made. A parson's table isn't well-made if the legs don't match up perfectly. All sides should be flush so that any paint or art work won't crack or split at these joining points. Well-made tables have a small block of wood glued to the underside where the legs have been set in. Of course it is rather difficult to judge quality when you're ordering furniture through the mail. However, if you have been looking at unfinished furniture in shops, you can usually make your selection according to style, price and written description.

Jon and I designed and executed all the pieces shown in this book, and we found that the problems varied from one piece to the next. We became quite experienced at correcting the imperfections that did exist. As I've already pointed out, we are not expert carpenters or cabinetmakers. So I pass along our findings as do-it-yourself craft workers who enjoy new challenges. It's in this spirit that I offer our hints, suggestions, and sometimes rather dogmatic conclusions about our experiences with the furniture presented here.

I am not making an attempt to teach refinishing or how to transform something artificial into something that looks authentic. We have applied our design concepts to show how different crafting techniques can be used to make unfinished furniture interesting, pretty, sometimes unusual and distinctive. Rather than attempting to show absolutely everything that can be done with unfinished pieces, I have been primarily concerned with revealing the range of clever uses of materials that are available to everyone. Since there is an initial outlay of money for the furniture, it would not make sense to spend a great deal for the crafting materials in order to achieve a spectacular effect. Therefore, for the most part, I have tried to keep the expenses to a minimum.

While I feel that most crafting experiences cannot be rushed, nor should they be, the projects presented here are designed to be finished in a short period of time—most of them in a day. Others will take longer only because I sometimes got carried away with the process and found ways to extend it. The raw furniture pieces, in themselves, are not unusual, but I would hope that our design ideas will spark your imagination so that you can transform your pieces, making them unique. However, if you want to execute any project exactly as it appears, it would be most disappointing if you were unable to get the furniture piece. Therefore, the projects are limited to furniture most readily available. I must admit that my love for old furniture tugged at me a bit. I would have

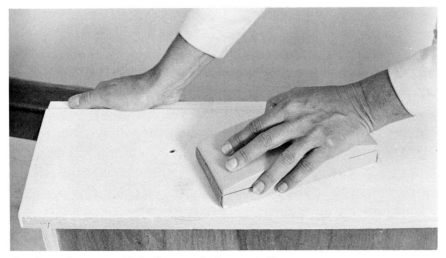

Sand surface smooth before and after painting.

enjoyed using some of these techniques and designs on a discarded "find" from a tag sale, but my sense of responsibility got the better of me. I would like to suggest, however, that if you have some interesting old furniture that needs redoing, it would make any of these projects all the more exciting. Sometimes the item you find needs work in the area of stripping off an old finish before adding the new. Others, such as the decoupage and most painting projects, require an overall sanding and a rubdown with some turpentine or paint thinner and that's it.

I have offered product suggestions for all the projects. This is not intended to imply that the only products that can be used are those that I have recommended. However, I have suggested what I have found to work best for me. There may be products that I haven't come across that are better for individual jobs. Whenever you have material on hand that you know will substitute well for something that I have recommended, use it. It is always best to make a test beforehand on a separate board just to be sure. When only a certain product will achieve the effects presented, then I have made that clear. In most cases I have tried several different ways and have presented what I consider to be the best, saving you the experience of experimental failures. But sometimes I have even let you know about these. Since I have worked with almost every craft technique I can become as stubborn as every other craftworker who is convinced that the tools he or she uses are the only ones for the job—only to find that the person sitting next to me is in total disagreement. Well, since I'm the one who is writing this book, I will pass along my experience and suggest that you follow the directions unless you feel adventurous enough to do a little experimenting on your own.

Recessed areas and defects in the wood can be corrected with wood filler.

## preparation of furniture

### sanding

To prepare raw wooden furniture for finishing it is best to begin by sanding all exposed areas. If the wood is very rough use a medium grade sandpaper such as a 220 grit. A hand sander is useful to own. This inexpensive item holds a strip of sandpaper, making the job easier while saving wear and tear on your hands. I prefer 3M WetorDry black sandpaper (grade 400) for finishing. When slightly wet this sandpaper makes a painted or varnished finish as smooth as satin. Always sand in the direction of the grain of the wood.

### shellac

Shellac is often used to seal the wood and act as a primer. Pure shellac dries quickly and has many advantages over varnish, the drying time being the major one. It also dries to a smooth finish unlike varnish which forms tiny bubbles on the surface. Once sanded almost all the furniture presented here was sealed with a coat of shellac. In order for shellac to be most effective it must be diluted with equal parts of denatured alcohol.

For many years all furniture was finished with a coat or two of shellac. It is easy to apply and looks pleasing. However, it is not the best substance to use as a final finish. One of the problems is that alcohol will dissolve it—the surface will become gummy if an alcoholic drink is accidentally spilled on a shellacked table top. Another problem is that a wet glass set on this surface will leave a white ring.

Since none of our unfinished furniture is left in the raw, shellac is used only as a sealer. It closes the pores of the wood so that several coats of paint or varnish are not necessary. Products on the market called "sealers" can successfully be used in place of shellac. However, sealer is usually white in color, not always good under a dark surface, and takes much longer to dry. It is also more expensive. Before deciding which sealer to use, decide what the project will be and what chemicals you will be using.

Unfortunately, I had one disaster. I thought it would be wise to sand and seal all the furniture at once so that it would be prepared for any project. The small rocker took longer than the rest to dry and I discovered that I had not "cut" the shellac with enough alcohol when covering it. The project required the use of acrylic paint which began to separate as it dried. It was not adhering to the sticky shellac surface. The paint had to be sanded off and the shellac removed with alcohol. The rocker was then primed with a coat of spray enamel paint to seal the wood before beginning again.

## paint

Painting unfinished furniture is probably the most popular way to finish it. Almost every kind of paint was used on one or another of the pieces and I still like the water base, fast-drying, indoor latex paint the best. However, in order to preserve this finish it must be covered with a coat of varnish.

Most furniture is painted with oil base enamel for a long-lasting finish, but it is messy, requires turpentine or paint thinner for cleanup, and smells terrible. I try to avoid using it unless the project requires a certain effect that can only be gotten with enamel paint. The Art Deco table was such a project. We wanted a very high gloss, hard finish in a deep wine color, so we bought a can of enamel paint.

The introduction of spray enamels has made everyone's life a little easier. They take only minutes longer to dry than latex or water base paint. Actually, almost all spray-painted projects are dry enough to sand in about one hour, and the surface is smooth and clean of brush strokes. Read the directions on the can. If you hold the can too close to the object you're spraying, drip marks will form which are difficult to sand off once dry. While these paints come in a wide range of colors, they are fairly standard and if you are trying to match or create a specific color it is not always easy to find the color in spray paint. Don't always go by the color on the can. Test the paint on a piece of scrap wood.

Almost any kind of paint can be used.

## varnish

Varnish does not really belong in this section on preparation since it is not a sealer but a finish. However, it is often mistaken for shellac and I thought this would be a good time to differentiate between them. While shellac is a fine sealer it is not a good finish. Varnish is everything shellac isn't. It is impervious to everything short of walking over it in golf shoes and when applied properly gives a beautifully smooth, lustrous finish to any surface. For our purposes indoor wood varnish is used in a glossy or matte satin finish. It is easy to apply once you get the knack of it and the most important thing is to let it dry for a full twenty-four hours. If you are using water base paint you will need a separate brush for varnishing as well as paint thinner to clean the brush.

Polyurethane is a relatively new product often used in place of varnish. This is a plastic resin and creates a tough surface. It is treated exactly the same as varnish and comes in both glossy and matte finishes. The high gloss is stronger and seems to dry in less time than the varnish, but I still give a coat a full day to dry. For children's furniture and those pieces that will get a lot of use, polyurethane is the perfect finish. When dry it can be sanded and then rubbed with steel wool for a smooth, glassy effect.

## stain

Stains are generally used to bring out the beauty of the wood grain or to emphasize the color. Minwax is a widely distributed brand name and is an excellent stain that comes in various wood tones. This type of sealer penetrates into the wood, rather than resting on the surface the way varnish does. It is extremely easy to use and the effects are overwhelming. You simply brush it over all the exposed wood areas and leave it alone for fifteen minutes. The stain will soak into the pores of the wood. Wipe away the excess stain and leave the piece to dry overnight. Even the worst-looking wood is enhanced with an application of stain. This can then be waxed and used as is. Or, once dry, two or three coats of varnish or polyurethane can be applied. When the varnish is dry it is rubbed with steel wool for a smooth finish.

You may decide to prepare your furniture piece with stain as a background before applying any of the crafting techniques. In that case, sand the wood smooth after the stain has dried. You may decide to apply another coat of stain to achieve a darker color. Remember though that the final varnishing will also darken and enrich the color. Complete the decoration and then apply clear varnish or polyurethane to the entire surface.

**stenciled dresser**

# stenciled dresser

Make my own stencil? Never! That was my first reaction when I decided that it would make a great project for one of the bureaus. Oh, sure, small letters or a simple design to go on a cube, but a design large enough to fit on a dresser was another matter. However, the idea seemed too good to pass up. Imagine the design potential if you could take any pattern and transfer it to a piece of furniture. Delightful wallpaper or fabric prints could be carried out to include the furniture, creating a totally integrated design concept for a room. Creating a clever design is one thing; painting a realistic representation is something else. In this case stenciling provides a terrific solution.

Stenciling involves applying color to the surface of an object through cut-out areas of paper. It has always been popular in this country, although it has been practiced in other countries as well, most notably Japan. We are probably most familiar with the stenciled designs of the Pennsylvania Dutch, the early American design motifs stenciled on Boston rockers, and, more recently, quilt designs stenciled on furniture and floors.

Stenciling is quite easy to do. The designs do not have to be limited to use on small pieces of furniture. In Europe during the early part of the nineteenth century expensive-looking "wallpaper" was actually a repeated stencil design. Aside from furniture, walls and floors, stenciling can be applied to fabric. A popular stenciled item many years ago was a canvas or oil cloth floor covering stenciled with an elaborate design, edged with an equally elaborate border. The effect was that of a very expensive carpet or floor painting.

Today the technique of stenciling is done just about the same way it was long ago. Simple designs can be done with one stencil, while more complex designs require a different stencil for each color. Many precut commercial stencils are on the market; however, these designs are limited and certainly not customized for your particular needs. In order to match another element in the room you must make your own —it's not difficult. Besides, it's a lot of fun.

If your room is wallpapered with a distinctive print or you have used an unusual fabric in the curtains or upholstery, why not create this exact design on a stenciled piece of furniture? No special talent is required and it will not take very long. If you like the design that I used on this dresser you can trace and use it on a three-drawer dresser as shown. Use the colors that best match the other elements in the room.

The materials used for this stencil project are available in art supply and hobby shops. They are: tracing paper; a pencil; a ruler; an X-acto knife; rubber cement; a 1-inch bristle brush; four shades of acrylic paint; varnish; sandpaper; white latex paint; a 2-inch paint brush; brush cleaner.

Prepare the dresser by sanding it with a medium grade sandpaper. Rough edges and imperfections should be smooth to the touch before painting. Wipe away sand grit and fill any gouges or irregular, depressed areas with wood putty. Elmer's wood filler has a water base and works well for this. It is not

Rough sketch of wallpaper design adapted to shape of dresser.

messy, can be applied with a putty knife and cleans with water. Let this dry overnight before sanding the surface so that it is even with the rest of the wood. The wood should then be sealed with shellac or a primer coat of paint.

A pale background color is usually best for a large piece. I used white latex wall paint. A 2-inch paint brush is most comfortable for applying paint directly from a can. Remove the drawers and paint them separately. Let the paint dry thoroughly before sanding the surface lightly with a fine grade sandpaper. If the piece requires another coat of paint, apply it and sand again when dry. Be sure that the furniture is clean and free of sand dust before applying your stencil.

For this dresser I used a bright, busy wallpaper from Waltex and blew up a section of the pattern. The poppies are the most appealing part of the design, but I wasn't sure how they would look in relation to the dresser drawers. If you have a wallpapered room, trace a few of the design elements so that you can get an idea of how they will look when removed from the overall pattern.

Begin by tracing a flower or two, then draw a rectangle around them to see if the design will look well. This can be

Finalize design, trace and make a grid. Each square equals 2 inches.

done rather crudely to approximate what the actual piece will look like. Fill in some color around the drawing to simulate the wallpaper in the background.

Next make a tighter tracing of the exact design elements and color them in with Magic Markers exactly the way you want them. This will help determine the colors to be used. This step is not absolutely necessary, but many people have difficulty determining what the finished piece will look like and this will certainly help. It also serves as a good reference while working. Add some leaves or other touches where you think they might be needed to complete the picture. Perhaps you want the design to extend up onto the top of the dresser as well as over onto the sides. Since this design was planned to dominate one side of the front, the leaves extend a bit over the top with only a few carried over to one side.

Make a grid of 2-inch squares and scale up the design to size. For this you need a piece of tracing paper the size of the

Coat back of tracing with rubber cement.

Cut through the outlined sections and remove the tracing paper.

bureau. Art supply stores often carry large pads of paper or you may be able to obtain it on a roll. If you cannot get the large size, tape several smaller pieces together to make a piece large enough for the project. Scale the artwork up by copying each square of the small design onto the larger grid. This bureau is 2 feet wide.

Coat the back of the tracing paper with rubber cement. Then lay a section at a time down on the bureau front. This is done most easily with the bureau lying down, face up. Since the tracing paper is so large it should be handled carefully. However, rubber cement does not make a permanent bond; if you make an error the paper can be easily lifted and placed down again. Smooth the paper out over the drawers and let the cement dry.

Peel away cut-out tracing pieces and save them for later use.

The next step is to cut through the outline of the design using a sharp X-acto knife or razor blade. First cut out the areas where two colors come together. In this case I cut away the blue and yellow centers of the flowers. Avoid carving into the furniture by using a gentle touch on the blade. It is not necessary to press hard as the tracing paper is very thin and a sharp blade will cut through it without any difficulty. Peel away these small cut-out pieces and save them—they'll be used again. Rub away the rubber cement from the surface of the bureau where you have just removed the paper. This can be done with your finger or a rubber cement pick-up. This inexpensive item, which looks like a square eraser, can be found in an art supply store. It is very handy to have as it will assure you of a clean surface.

Acrylic paints are used for this project; they coat well, although they are very rubbery (more about this difficulty later). They can be purchased in tubes from an art supply store.

Spread a piece of the wallpaper in front of you so that you can check your colors while mixing. This should be done care-

Apply correct paint colors to each separate area.

fully. Mismatching colors will stand out on such a large area, so take the time to get them as closely matched as possible. Of course if you aren't copying a design the colors simply need to be pleasing and appropriate for the area in which the dresser will be used. A palette knife and a piece of waxed paper or cardboard are good for mixing. Once you are sure of the mixture, whip up what you think you'll need in a small cup or jar. This design requires a lot of green paint, but only a small amount of yellow and blue. For the large red poppies use Grumbacher poppy red right from the tube. Also, be sure to buy a tube of white paint. There is bound to be some error that needs to be corrected around the outline of the design. Be prepared! It's also good to have the white for mixing with other colors.

Cut out all large areas, such as the green leaves and stems, and remove the rubber cement before painting. Then, using a stiff 1-inch brush, paint in from the edges to the center to avoid getting paint under the edge of the paper. Although the tracing paper is secure on the dresser, there may be some loose edges and if the paint slips under them the design will smudge.

Next cut out the large red poppies and again remove the rubber cement before painting. Replace the cut-out tracing pieces over the yellow and blue centers (or any other area of your design where one color meets another). This is done to prevent paint from getting onto the already-painted areas.

When you finish an area in one color, don't throw away the extra mixed paint until the entire piece is finished and you have a chance to stand back and look it over. If you need to tone down a color that's too bright, add a darker color to the original paint and apply it with a small, pointed artist's brush.

When the entire design has been painted, check to see if any areas need a second coat. This should be done before removing the stencil or you will have no outline to follow. Work quickly as it is best to remove the tracing paper while the paint is slightly wet. I mentioned before that acrylic paint covers well, although it becomes rubbery. The problem is that, when dry, it can easily be lifted off with the tracing paper. Therefore for best results when removing the stencil, gently pull it away from the painted surface rather than tearing it off in one direction.

Remove all the tracing paper and clean the rubber cement away from entire surface. If you want to add more to the design at this time, such as to the top or sides, this can easily be done by placing the desired stencilled area where you want this added touch.

Touch up spots that need it with the paint you saved. Using the white, touch up any smudged edges. This is best done with a small, stiff brush.

Pull out the drawers and paint the top edges where the design falls. There should be no gaps between drawers. Fill in where needed to finish off the design. When you are satisfied with the results let the paint dry thoroughly.

For a long-lasting protective finish, coat the entire piece of furniture with glossy polyurethane. Remove the drawers to do this and let the finish dry overnight. You may find that two coats are desirable. If there are tiny bumps in the dried surface go over this with a fine piece of steel wool. Wipe away the particles and wax the furniture with clear paste wax.

Touch up smudged areas with white paint.

Replace the original drawer knobs—or you might want to look around for decorative ones that seem appropriate. Wooden knobs can be painted so that they are camouflaged into the design.

A friend of mine stenciled a bureau for her little girl's room and continued the design onto the floor. It is very effective. However, the bureau can never be placed in any other spot in the room because the leaves from the flowers flow right from the bottom of the dresser onto the floor. Nevertheless, it is a cute idea—especially for a small room.

# suede-covered parson's table

# suede-covered parson's table

Parson's tables have got to be the best idea sold in unfinished furniture. The basic square design is good-looking and the table is versatile. Almost every magazine you pick up has at least one parson's table, painted or covered, somewhere in a decorator room setting—coming in unobtrusively from the corner of the page perhaps, or adding color somewhere in the background, but usually there. These tables have been used so often that they have become standard in most rooms. Yes, right alongside the most expensive furniture and fabrics.

Another advantage these tables have is their ability to fill a need, or spot, immediately. Just pick one up and plunk it down and it fits in. However, the creative potential is another thing. You can do everything and anything to them. We have painted them, stained them, covered them with fabric, paper, tile, and tape—and they always look good. They are even terrific left in the raw.

Whatever you decide to do with yours this is one area where you should look for quality. If the legs aren't flush with the sides you will have trouble once you have completed the project. It is at this point that paint will crack, fabric will bulge, and decoupage cut-out designs will surely split. The only time that this doesn't matter is when covering the entire table with tough vinyl wallcovering. If you can't find really well-made parson's tables be prepared to do a little reinforcing on your own. Fill in cracks with wood putty and sand so that all areas fit flush. Use a wood plane if necessary. By and large, most of these tables are well-made, but it is good to be cautious. The better ones don't cost much more than those made poorly.

I am often asked where design ideas for craft projects come from. Everywhere. Sometimes it is something mentioned in a conversation. Often it is a combination of experiences and visual images. Since we are all different and have our own experiences, the designs that we create are unique. We also draw on the design ideas of others. And we all have different tastes, which determines choice.

The more involved with crafting you are, the easier it is

to keep thinking of new ideas since one usually leads to another. I always find that right in the middle of doing a project I think of an idea and file it away for another time. In a way that's what happened with this suede-covered table.

For this project you will need: an 18-inch parson's table; approximately ½ yard of each color suede cloth (buy a little extra for error); Spra-Ment adhesive; a straightedge; a razor blade or X-acto knife; sheet of 2-inch stencil letters; white acrylic paint; a stipple brush; Scotchgard (optional).

Each piece of fabric should hang over front edge.

Slice through overlapping layers of fabric.

Peel away excess material.

Lay the straightedge diagonally across the table top from corner to corner. Draw a straight line and then another at right angles, making an "X." Cut out four triangles using the table top as a guide, (two in sand, two in rust.) These pieces can be cut rather crudely with scissors. They should be oversized, large enough to hang past the front edge of the table. Turn the fabric pieces face down on a large piece of scrap paper. Spray liberally with Spra-Ment adhesive being careful not to get any on the front (it is very sticky). Lay each piece of suede on the table so that the colors alternate. They will overlap.

The best part about using suede is that there are no frayed edges. Therefore, when gluing the pieces in place there are no edges to fold under and the finish will be smooth. This is also an advantage when doing the precision cutting.

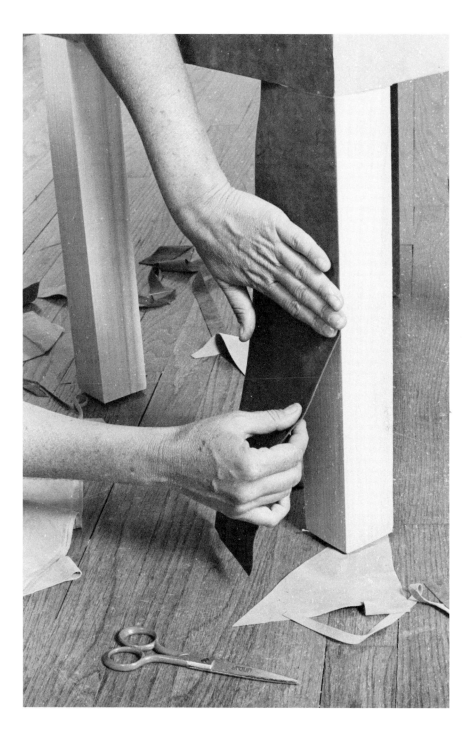

Smooth the fabric down on the table top. Press the creased edges and smooth the fabric down over the front edges of the table as well. The fabric can be trimmed at the corners with a razor blade. Tuck the suede cloth under the table's edge for a finished look.

Place the metal ruler across the top of the fabric from corner to corner and slice through the material with a sharp

Trace words and center on the table.

razor blade. If it is difficult to go through all the layers that are overlapped, run the blade across again. Peel away the excess fabric. This will lift easily. Follow the same procedure on the other side. The two colors of fabric should butt together perfectly.

The legs are covered with the two contrasting colors. After deliberating over making them one solid color or two, this solution seemed to look best. The front and inside of each leg correspond to the triangle color. For each leg, cut two strips wide enough to wrap around and cover two sides. These pieces can overlap slightly or you can cut them so that they butt together at the corners. Spray the pieces with adhesive and apply them. Once all the material is adjusted on the table you might want to run a rubber brayer over the edges.

Each letter must be dry before continuing onto the next.

Decide on the words that you want to use for the top of the table. Of course you don't have to use ours. Stencil the outline of the words in pencil on a piece of scrap paper. Use this to center each word on the table. Place the stenciled word on one side so that it is exactly where you want it. Put the first letter of the plastic stencil sheet over the penciled letter and slide the paper out from under it. This is where you will begin. Hold the stencil on the fabric with one hand. Gingerly dip the stipple brush into the white paint (you want very little paint on the brush). The stenciling is done by tapping the paint onto the fabric within the stencil letter. Each letter must be absolutely dry before going onto the next or you will smudge it. While you are waiting for this letter to dry, turn the table and begin the first letter of each successive word.

When all the words have been stenciled onto the table and are completely dry, you can give everything a protective coating of Scotchgard. This is not the same as Spra-Ment. It is a soil-resistent treatment, only recommended if you feel it is needed.

While our table is covered with suede cloth, there are many other ways that this same idea could have been carried out. Perhaps you have some soft leather or canvas or other sturdy fabric that will work just as well. It should not, however, be too fragile or require any edge seaming.

# mirrored cube table

# mirrored cube table

Wallpaper was the inspiration for this project which would be perfect in a young girl's room. Striped or bordered paper is excellent to cut apart, creating a more interesting effect than simply covering the cube with a solid pattern. This project is extremely easy and we completed it in one morning. Spray paint helped. Often it's disappointing to find that the color you want to match isn't available in a spray paint. Then you must get involved with mixing your own paints (not always easy) or having the color mixed (expensive if you're only covering a small area). So choose your paper carefully according to available spray paint colors.

The cube, which comes from the J. C. Penney catalog, is the only one we found with one recessed side. Actually sold as a storage cube, this side is meant to be placed against the wall. While this side is not sturdy enough to sit on it's perfect as the top of a night table. A glass can be set into this space or, as in this case, a 12-inch square mirror. These mirrors are available in wallcovering and decorating shops or through J. C. Penney's catalog. Intended as wallcovering, these mirrors have many terrific uses. Four can be placed on the top of a 24-inch parson's table to make an interesting dining table. The legs and sides can be finished with a coat of silver spray paint or covered with silver Mylar or Contact paper. The mirror used for this project has a dark smoky tint, but they are also available in clear glass.

The materials needed are: one 16-inch wooden cube with one recessed side; Krylon spray paint (we used hot pink); sandpaper; wood filler (if needed); a small putty knife; Krylon spray varnish; Waltex vinyl wallpaper; Elmer's Glue-All; a razor blade or X-acto knife; a straightedge; a 12-inch square mirror; 15-inch by 20-inch illustration board.

Sand the cube smooth on all sides. Since these cubes do not come assembled you will have to screw the sides together; the instructions are very clear and the process is simple. The recessed areas where the screws are should be filled with wood filler. Borden's makes a very good water base filler and a small can goes a long way. It can be applied with a small

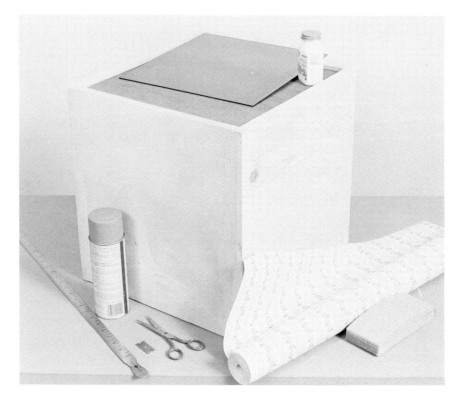

Cut through overlapping pieces to miter corners.

putty knife or similar utensil. It takes a few hours for the putty to dry, so it is a good idea to do the preparation for this project the day before. Once dry, sand the puttied areas so they are smooth and even with the wooden surface.

Spray all four sides and the top rim with paint. Do this outside if possible, or in a well ventilated room. Two or three coats are required. This paint dries very quickly and you can

Drawing outline of mirror on illustration board.

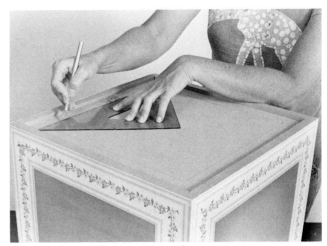

Use X-acto knife to cut board.

Mount illustration board frame onto glued surface.

Set mirror into position.

spray one coat on top of another within twenty minutes. When dry, sand the paint very lightly with 400 grade sandpaper. Wipe away sand dust.

Measure the cube from top to bottom to determine the length of the wallpaper strips to be cut. Sometimes a 16-inch cube varies slightly in measurement. Cut sixteen strips of wallpaper, each slightly longer than the cube. Turn the cube on its side and lay the strips in place. Hold the two that come together at the corner and place the metal ruler over the paper from the corner tip to the inside corner where the paper meets. Make a mitered corner by cutting it with a razor blade at this point as shown in the photograph. Repeat this process on all sides where the paper meets. Spread Elmer's glue on the back of each strip as it is used and place it on the

Cover frame with wallpaper strips.

side of the cube. Each piece should match perfectly, creating a frame on all four sides of the table.

Measure the recessed area of the cube and cut a square this size from single weight illustration board (available in art supply stores). Place the mirror in the center of this board and draw a square around it. Cut this out using a razor blade or X-acto knife.

Spread glue over the top of the cube and place the cut-out illustration board piece into the recess. Press it down firmly. Place the mirror in the center and press it down onto the glued surface. The mirror will be set into the frame you have just created. Cut strips of wallpaper to fit around the mirror on the illustration board. Glue and cut them the same way you did the sides.

To protect the sides and top edges spray them with Krylon clear varnish. Three coats will cover well and the finish will be shiny. This is not absolutely necessary, but if you have already purchased the varnish for another project, use it here. Sand lightly and wax.

# wallpapered night table

# wallpapered night table

When a piece is really lovely it is difficult to paint or cover it; you feel a responsibility to preserve the basic good qualities that exist to begin with. This was definitely not the case with the little night stand. In fact when I first saw it I thought, "How ugly." I must admit that I wasn't overly excited about working on it, but I couldn't find one that was nicer. I was afraid that this time a project would get short shrift. However, it isn't any fun to begin a project with that attitude. I have done so many craft projects that began with a nonchalant shrug, only to have them end up becoming some of my favorites. This kind of project is labeled as a challenge; it's a nice situation to be in because it gives you the opportunity to call on all your creativity.

Tacked up on my studio wall are samples of delightful wallpaper designs created by Laura Ashley for The Raintree Collection. Each has a corresponding fabric and the designs have been used extensively in decorating. I wanted to use this paper for crafting. The wine-colored printed design is quite elegant—just the opposite in feeling from the night stand. "Why not give it some status?" I thought. Covering this piece with paper isn't a very unique crafting idea, unless you use great-looking paper. But, in order to add a touch of our own, Jon and I decided to apply a detail using the technique of wood burning. This is not difficult and turned out to be great fun. A wood burning pen can be found in hobby and toy stores for about five dollars. The set comes with a variety of tips for different designs. The tiny triangles of the paper seemed perfect to duplicate on the drawer front. Since the paper has a dark background and white designs, the dark wood-burned pattern seemed appropriate against the natural wood. When doing this project choose a paper or fabric design that is appropriate for a repeat wood-burning design.

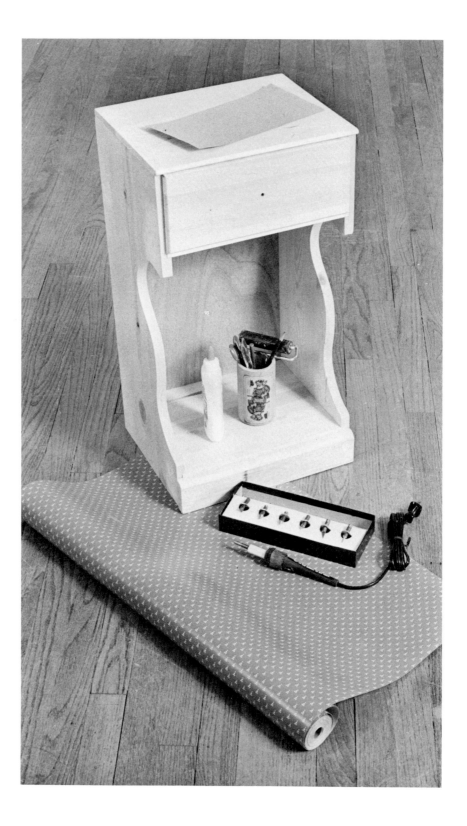

The materials needed for this are: a wooden night table; wallpaper (available from Philan Distributors, N.Y.); a large bottle of Elmer's Glue-All; scissors; a razor blade; a pencil; a sponge; a ruler; a staple gun (optional); and a wood burning pen.

Begin by cutting out all the pieces of paper. To do this, lay

Smooth the glued paper onto the front edges. The cuts in the paper will eliminate folds or wrinkles.

each side of the table down on the wallpaper and draw around the outline with a pencil. Leave an extra inch or so at the back and bottom so that the paper can be folded back and stapled or glued. Don't scrimp—excess can always be trimmed with a blade. Cut this out and use it as a pattern for the other three sides. Remember to cut the interior side pieces smaller so that they fit. If you have chosen a small, overall pattern, there is no concern about matching. However, if you are using a design that must be matched, then you must take extra care in cutting out each piece. Cut strips for the front edge, wide enough to overlap on each side.

Apply glue liberally to the front edges of the table and cover onto one inch of each side using a damp one-inch sponge

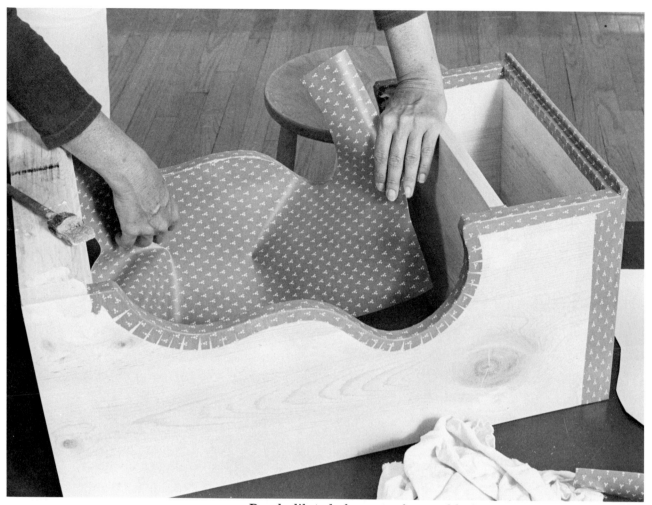

Brush diluted glue onto the wood before attaching cut-out pieces.

brush. The sponge brush helps to dilute the glue and makes spreading it easier.

Hold a paper strip in one hand and place it at the top of the front curve. With the other hand smooth the paper down the front of the curved edge. Be sure this top part is smooth and secure. With straight scissors make a cut in from the edge of the paper every half inch. Do this on both sides as it will allow you to glue the side strips flat with no folds or wrinkles in the paper. Pat the strips down with a cloth or damp sponge. This will also remove any excess glue that may ooze out from the edges.

Place the table on its side and coat the exposed wood with slightly diluted glue. Brushing the glue across the piece will

assure an even coating. Lay the cut-out side piece of paper in
place on the table and smooth it down all over. Make sure as
you do this that all edges are lined up. If the paper is a bit
larger than the side, the excess can be trimmed with a sharp
razor blade once the paper is dry. Continue to cover all exposed areas in this way. Do not cover the drawer, but do cut
out a piece for it. Keep this piece separate.

The paper that you have folded to the back can now be
secured with a staple gun. If you don't have this tool, simply
glue the edges to the back of the table as you did with the
sides. Turn the table upside down and staple the bottom. The
stapling procedure is not absolutely necessary as the glue
alone will hold the paper. The stapling merely adds to the
table's durability.

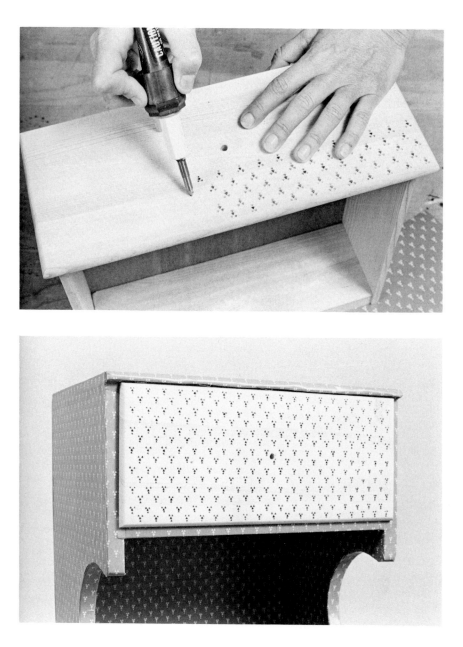

The wallpaper used here is heavy, water-resistant vinyl and needs no protective coating. If you use a more fragile paper, a coat or two of varnish should be applied to protect the surface. If your piece is covered with fabric, it is a good idea to spray it with Scotchgard to make it soil-resistant.

Tape the cut-out pattern onto the front of the drawer with masking tape. For this small design we used a pushpin to designate the areas to be burned. Prick through the paper into the wood at the exact spot where the wood burning pen will repeat the design. Do this on the entire drawer. Remove the taped paper and make your burn marks. The pen will get very hot as you use it. Do not hold it too close to the point. This is not a child's toy even though it's sold in toy stores. Read the enclosed directions before using it.

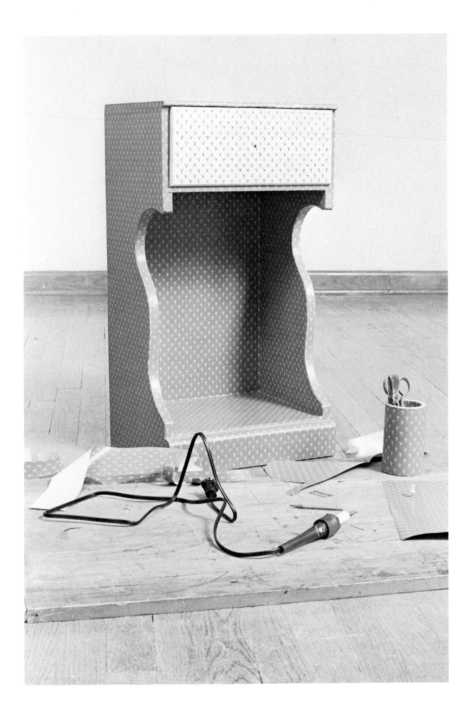

We discovered that it's a good idea to first try the pen on an extra piece of wood since it takes awhile to get the knack. The designs will also be more accurate if you practice doing them first. Once you get going it's easy and the more you do the better it looks. For a first project the drawer is just about the right size. It is a lot of fun but the burning takes time to do well, so don't make doing the entire table your first project.

A coat of varnish will protect the wood and give it a finished look.

# gourd print dresser

## gourd print dresser

I've found the perfect marriage! It's between a three-drawer dresser and posters from the New York Botanical Garden. I first discovered these fabulous posters when I was working on a project for a magazine. The huge sunflower poster was perfect for the top of an electrical spool turned coffee table. I wrote and ordered several more and that was the beginning of a long love affair. Of course there are posters sporting every subject imaginable available all over the country but these posters in particular are delicate and livable. By that I mean you can place them in almost any room and they will be beautiful. I never seem to tire of them. And for a three-drawer dresser measuring 24 by 14 by 28 inches you have a perfect match. Ordering information for posters is available from the New York Botanical Garden, Bronx, N.Y. 10458.

The design used on this dresser is a continuous vine of gourds which has been cut apart and made to fit over the drawers. The stems extend a bit here and there to leave enough to flow up and onto the top. This is an easy project and can be completed in just a few hours.

If you're not familiar with decoupage, it's a French word meaning "to cut out". Years ago the French and Italians decorated furniture with elaborately cut paper designs that were covered with a lacquered finish. Several coats of lacquer were applied until the paper designs were completely submerged and the surface was smooth as glass.

Today this craft has become popular with professional as well as amateur craftworkers and all craft and hobby shops carry the necessary supplies to do everything from a small box or plaque right up to a piece of furniture. Since I have been doing decoupage practically all my life there is almost nothing that has escaped my scissors and varnish brush. Faced with a raw piece of furniture and a beautiful botanical print it doesn't take me two seconds to decide that decoupage is the solution. It is one of the nicest ways I know to decorate an object that will be used and displayed.

To begin working on the dresser, first prime it as suggested in the introductory section. It is especially important

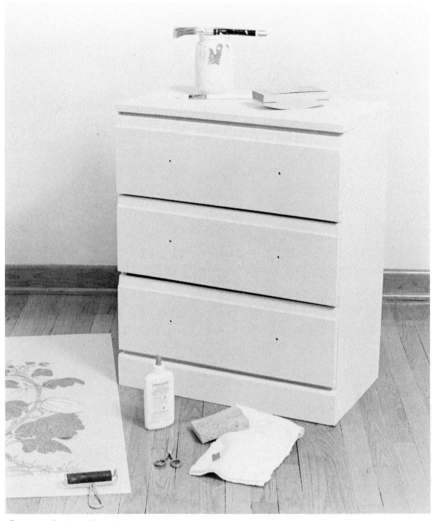
Large design has been cut from a poster.

with a piece that will be decoupaged to do a good sanding and painting job. The hand sander makes the sanding go quickly; be sure to smooth out any defects so that the design will not appear lumpy. Most experts recommend a good indoor enamel paint for furniture, but since you will be covering this piece with many coats of varnish enamel isn't necessary. For this project I used a flat latex indoor wall paint. It's easy to use, cleans quickly and dries before you can turn around to wash out your brush.

If you want a colored background, the easiest and cheapest way to mix the shade you want is with a small amount of acrylic paint mixed into the latex white. I always buy a gallon of white paint so that I can mix my own colors for all my projects. The acrylic paints come in every color imaginable and are easily found in art supply stores. Pour a generous amount of the white paint into a clean jar. Squirt a very small amount of the acrylic paint into the jar and, using a wooden paint stick, combine the two. The acrylic colors are usually

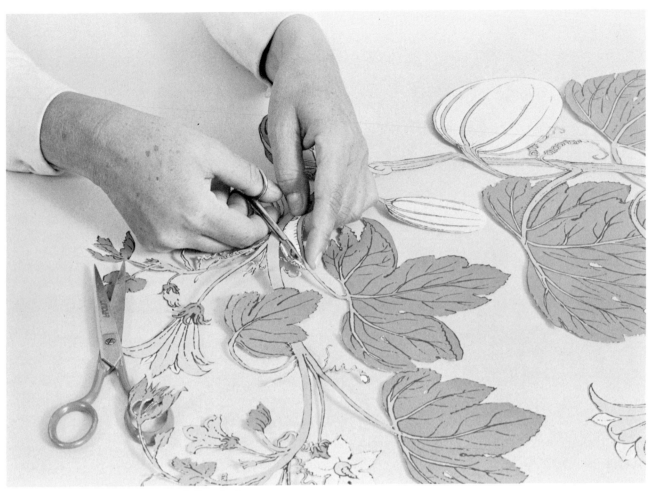

Cut away excess paper around the design.

quite intense therefore add only a drop at a time to achieve
a very pale color. The dresser here is painted a soft, creamy
yellow. When using a pastel paint two coats are usually necessary to achieve a complete cover. Sand lightly between coats
using a number 320 sandpaper grit. I find that 3M sandpaper
is the best.

While the paint is drying you can begin to cut out the
poster design. The reason for cutting away the background is
to make the design seem as though it is part of the piece of
furniture, as though it had been painted on the surface. It is
important with decoupage to cut away the excess paper as
carefully as possible. The better the cutting the more professional the finished results will be. If the background paint is
white then the cutting job can be less perfect. However, if you
use a colored background the white paper that is left between
the stems and leaves will show up and detract from the overall effect.

Begin by cutting away all the outer paper with good size

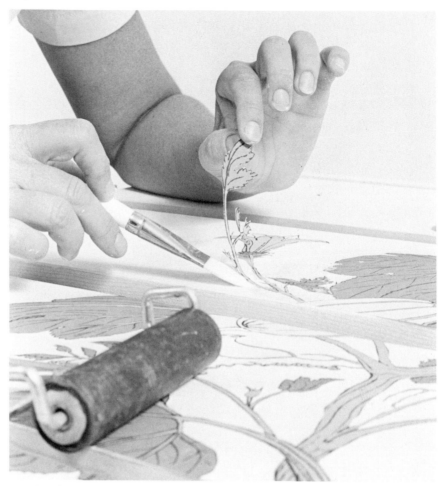

Apply glue with a paint brush.

scissors—a pair that is comfortable, such as kitchen scissors. When you get into the close, delicate areas, cuticle scissors work best. Because the blade is curved you can manipulate them to cut around curved areas. Take your time cutting. This step is difficult to rush and is best left for moments of relaxation.

Cutting can be fun and it is always satisfying to watch the design come alive as more and more of the background is stripped away. Cutting around the largest areas, such as leaves, rather than delicate stems is easiest. If you do this first the bulk of the design won't be weighing on the stems and there will be less chance of breaking at weak points. As more and more of the design is cut out it should be handled carefully to avoid losing a tiny leaf or bud. A large sheet of poster board is excellent for holding and transporting the work from one spot to another. If the design is not cut out, simply used as a poster, the outline of the poster's edges will show on the finished piece. Also, the design flexibility will be lost.

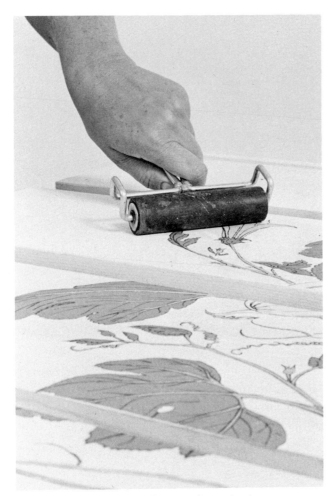

A brayer is used to roll over the cutout.

Each piece lines up with the one above it.

Once completely cut out the design can be positioned. You might find that if you cut away one of the flowers or leaves it can be placed elsewhere. Perhaps the sides or top could use some decoration as well as the front. If you do this, cut away extra pieces at points where it will appear natural.

Gluing a delicate design to dresser drawers can be quite tricky. Lay the dresser down with the drawers facing up. Place the completed cutout over the face of the dresser and begin to manipulate it until it fits the way you would like it to appear. Remember that when the spaces are cut apart between the drawers each piece of the design must line up with the one above. Part of the cutout is glued between the drawers to eliminate any separations and make the design look like one piece. There should be no choppy, uneven spaces. This is not difficult, but does take some concentration, so go slowly and do it right. Once finished it can't be redone. The glue is permanent.

Begin with the bottom strip of the front. Once this is

Coat entire dresser with polyurethane varnish.

secure it will be easier to move upward, cutting and gluing with no fear of the design getting out of line. Elmer's Glue-All is perfect. It dries clear, washes off your hands and dresser and bonds permanently. I find that if it is watered down slightly it remains strong and is much easier to use for this purpose.

Have a cup of water and a damp sponge within reach. Use a one-inch brush dipped in the water to spread the glue. Lift a section of the cutout and squirt a few drops of glue onto the dresser. With the wet brush spread the glue lavishly, covering all areas where the design will be placed. Press the section of the cutout down on the sticky surface and pat in place with the damp sponge. Often a rubber brayer, or roller, is a handy

Brush antiquing over a section at a time.

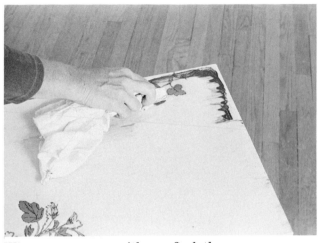
Wipe away excess with a soft cloth.

Traces of antiquing mix create a smoky effect.

Wax dresser after final varnishing.

tool for this process. The brayer is available in craft or art supply stores and is used to secure the paper cutout to the surface. If there are any edges that are not sufficiently glued in place, simply lift the paper and touch a spot of glue to it. With the sponge pat away any excess glue that may have oozed out from under the design when being rolled.

Curved areas will require special attention. A butter knife or screw driver can be used to smooth down the cutout in these hard-to-reach areas. Be sure that each new piece lines up with the one under and above it. A razor blade can be used to slice the paper under each drawer so that you can move the rest of the design up to the next section to be glued in place.

As you handle and glue the pieces keep your hands clean. This may sound like a silly thing to remind you of, but if there is any glue on your fingers you run the risk of having the design stick to you and ripping where it shouldn't.

When the gluing is completed, check your work. Be sure that you have left no unsecured edges. With the damp sponge pat over every part of the cutout to remove all excess glue. Sometimes if glue is left to dry on the surface this section will become slightly discolored under the varnish.

I described decoupage as having a lacquered finish when done in the eighteenth century. I have also been talking about a varnished finish. There is a difference. When lacquer was used there was no varnish. Today we use varnish for a hard, smooth, impenetrable surface and it can be applied as a high gloss or satin matte finish. When it is allowed to dry thoroughly nothing can ruin a varnished surface short of very strong paint remover.

Another relatively new finish is polyurethane, which I've described before as a plastic resin impervious to everything. I find it to be stronger than varnish and slightly clearer. Varnish tends to have an orange tint even when the can states that it is absolutely clear. Polyurethane is available in all hardware stores; I used one that produces a high gloss finish. This has a stronger odor than varnish and should be applied where there is good ventilation. If you are using varnish any brand is fine as long as it states specifically that it is for indoor wood use.

Apply the varnish or polyurethane to all exposed areas of the dresser. Remove the drawers and coat the front and sides of the front panel that will be exposed when replaced in the dresser. Always use a seperate brush for this. The paint brush is cleaned in water; the varnish brush in paint thinner, turpentine or mineral spirits.

A thin coat of varnish or polyurethane is better than glopping on a thick layer which will drip and bubble while drying. Start in the middle of the dresser or drawer and draw your brush from one side to the other. In this way the varnish becomes thinner as you reach the edges. Lightly draw the brush back the other way across the surface. Then leave it alone. This procedure cannot be rushed. The finish must dry a full day or overnight before sanding and applying another coat. If the process is rushed you will end up with a gummy, soft surface rather than a hard, smooth one.

During the drying time dust may settle on the surface causing small bumps. These are easily sanded away once the surface is completely dry. It will take approximately five coats to sufficiently cover the design and dresser so that it is smooth to the touch. If you prefer to have the design submerged under the varnish so that it is level with the dresser's surface more coats of varnish will be needed. With each coat the design becomes less raised.

Once three coats of varnish have been applied, the entire surface, cutout and all, is sanded lightly with fine 400 grit sandpaper. Use a light touch. If you find that part of the design is beginning to sand away either you are sanding too heavily or you will need another coat of varnish before continuing. Between coats of varnish keep your brush in mineral spirits or brush cleaner. This will keep it clean and soft and ready to use again. When you are finished clean the brush thoroughly and wrap it in cellophane to protect it for later use.

This bureau is accented with antiquing. It has been applied sparingly around the edges of the design and corners of drawers and bureau edge. To achieve this subtle effect mix equal parts oil base raw umber, linseed oil, and paint thinner or turpentine. This produces a warm, earth tone. If you prefer, you can use a premixed antiquing solution available in hardware and hobby stores in the color of your choice.

Using a small ½-inch brush casually apply the antiquing here and there, then wipe away most of it leaving only a trace of color where desired. A clean, soft cloth such as cheesecloth wrapped around your finger is perfect for this. Rub away most of the excess color leaving the rest around the design edges. It is easy to do this but you will have to work at it before getting a feeling for how much looks well. Do not leave streaks of antiquing across the design.

Stand back after applying the antiquing to one section so that you can determine the effect you wish to achieve. If you do one small area at a time it will allow you to work slowly and carefully. The antiquing set dries very quickly but should be left undisturbed for several hours so that it can dry thoroughly. Since it has an oil base it will smear if touched before fully dry. If you cannot find a tube of oil base raw umber, it does come in acrylic and should be thinned with a little water before using. I prefer the oil, but the acrylic is a good substitute. A drop of antiquing can be applied to corners as well as around the design, but again very lightly. This soft accent is very appealing if not too obvious. It rounds out and tones down the boldness and gives the piece a bit of character.

Let the antiquing dry and then apply a coat of varnish or polyurethane over all. Once again, this should dry overnight. In the morning the bureau will be ready for a final sanding. This is done as follows: In a cup mix a little water with a lot of soap until the water is very soapy. Dunk a small piece of

400 WetorDry sandpaper into the water until it is very wet. Then sand the entire bureau, rewetting the sandpaper as needed. Wipe away the sand grit and water with a clean cloth. This application will leave your piece absolutely satin smooth to the touch. For extra smoothness, rub the piece once again with 0000 steel wool. Wipe away the particles when you are finished and coat the bureau with Butcher's bowling alley wax. Let this sit for ten minutes, then rub and buff for a glowing finish. This wax will protect the furniture and can be reapplied every two or three months.

For an extra touch you might consider lining the drawers with wallpaper or Contact paper in a corresponding color or design. For added protection the lining can be given a coat or two of varnish.

# stained dresser

Probably the easiest way to finish a piece is with stain. The results are immediate and any wood tone can be achieved. All hardware stores carry a variety of stains and have sample wood pieces to show the effect of each. Aside from the authentic wood tones such as cherry, walnut, pine and mahogany, you can get a variety of colored stains such as red, green and mustard.

Wood stain comes in water or oil base, although I only recommend using one with an oil base. As a matter of fact, this is an area where I have yet to run into any controversy. Minwax is the only stain that I use, although I have tried others and even made my own concoction.

The only preparation for a stained finish is pre-sanding. If the wood needs some patching with wood filler do it carefully. Don't be too generous with the filler as it is difficult for the stain to penetrate. Let the filler dry thoroughly before sanding it smooth.

A deep, rich walnut tone is used here to enhance the wood grain. Mix the stain well before applying it. I have found that a sponge brush works best. Brush the stain back and forth across the bureau so that it is covered liberally. Sometimes this can be messy, especially when going down the sides, so place newspaper under the bureau before starting. The stain will soak into the wood penetrating and sealing it. Leave it for fifteen minutes; then, with a dry cloth, rub away the excess stain. Let the dresser dry overnight.

The print used for this project is another from the New York Botanical Garden print series. It is called Pomona Franconica. Cut away all of the surrounding white paper. For the large areas use regular straight scissors. Cuticle scissors are more accurate and easy to handle for the refined cutting.

When cut out the print will fit perfectly on the front of a 24 by 14 by 28-inch dresser. I wanted to extend it a bit so trimmed the heavy stem and cut it apart to make it longer. This can be done with almost any print that doesn't fit exactly as you would like. Adjust it to fit your needs.

As with the previous project, glue and secure the cutout

firmly with Elmer's Glue-All. Roll over the design either with a rubber brayer or rolling pin and remove excess glue with a damp sponge. Coat the entire piece with satin polyurethane varnish. This finish will make the walnut stain rich and lustrous. The first two coats will simply sink into the wood. However, if you apply two or three more coats the piece will have a strong, satin-smooth finish. Let each coat dry completely. That means overnight. I know I've said this before, but it is extremely important that it dry to insure a hard, beautiful finish. Rub over the wood between the last two coats and after the final coat with fine 0000 steel wool. Wipe away particles and wax. The color will glow.

# outdoor garden table

Early in the spring when the flowers are beginning to appear I always have the urge to collect and press them. Some flowers press better than others because they hold their shape and color. Ferns are especially beautiful, but my favorites are the buttercups. They retain their bright, yellow color indefinitely. Even the leaves are delicate and look pretty when pressed. I have used pressed flowers and leaves in all kinds of crafting projects and am constantly looking for new ways to display them. This project fits the bill perfectly.

The flowers you press for this project might be from your own garden or mementos from your travels. While the project is the easiest in the book and takes little time to complete, the flowers must be pressed at least two weeks before you are actually ready to begin. Collect a variety so that you have enough to choose from. Sometimes one leaf or fern is enough and looks well by itself. But if you want to create an arrangement you'll need many small pieces to try together. The buttercups for this table came from a field in back of my house, but the small leaves were picked in my grandmother's yard in Florida over a year ago.

The wallpaper used to cover the cube is washable vinyl Waltex in an overall fern pattern. There is no matching to do at the sides as this is one continuously repeating design. The framed border is made with Mystik tape which comes in a variety of colors.

The cube used for this is, again, the kind with one recessed side available from J. C. Penney. It is not strong enough to hold anything heavy but works perfectly as a small table to hold lightweight objects. The glass preserves the flowers underneath and is easily set into the top of the cube. You can even change the arrangement from time to time.

The materials needed are few. They include: enough wallpaper to cover four sides of the cube with one continuous piece; a razor blade; Elmer's glue; a variety of pressed flowers; single weight illustration board; one roll of yellow Mystik plastic tape and one roll of green each ¾-inch wide; a 16-inch wooden cube.

Use straightedge and razor blade to cut wallpaper.

Measure and cut one piece of wallpaper long enough to wrap around the cube. Spread glue down one edge of one side. Line the paper up with the top of the cube and press it down on the glue. Spread the glue evenly over the next side. It will flow more easily if you dilute the glue slightly with water and spread it with a sponge brush. Smooth the paper over the glued surface. You can use your hand or a wallpaper brush if you have one. Be sure that the air bubbles are pushed out to the edges as you do this. Turn the cube and apply glue to the next side and continue this process until each side is covered with paper. Be sure to line up the paper at the top of each edge before securing it with glue. If there is any paper left over it can be removed with a razor blade.

A piece of illustration board serves as the background on top (or the top of the cube could be painted). Cut the illustration board and set it into the recess. This provides a smooth surface for your design. In order to space the Mystik tape, cut a ¾-inch piece of cardboard. Lay this down on the inside edge of the top and make a pencil mark. Place it going down the

stenciled dresser

mirrored cube table

suede-covered parson's table

outdoor garden table

gourd print dresser

**scalloped coffee table**

**stained dresser**

**art deco table**

wallpapered night table

suede and tile table

hearts and ticking dresser

painted rocking chair

ivy plant stand

paper patchwork blanket chest

modular storage cubes

child's block table

burlap wine rack holder

fanciful stool and storage cube

flowered fabric dresser

ceramic tile table

tulip-covered table

Miter tape at corners.

side the other way and make another mark. Cut a piece of green tape and carefully adhere it where the pencil marks indicate. Each piece of tape will overlap at the corners. Next make a border of yellow retaining a ¾-inch white space between the yellow and green borders. Then edge the rim of the cube with green tape. Place a metal straightedge diagonally across each taped corner and slice through it with a razor blade. Peel away the excess tape and you will have a neatly mitered corner.

Arrange the pressed flowers and leaves within the framed area that you have created. Tweezers are helpful here. Keep the design elements within the same space, leaving a white area around the focal point. Try different arrangements until

A spot of glue here and there will keep flowers in place.

you are satisfied with the final design. Then lift each flower off one at a time and place a spot or two of glue underneath to secure the pressed pieces and prevent them from moving when you place the glass over the design.

The glass covering is simply the ordinary window pane variety which you can have cut wherever you buy it. Take the exact measurements or, better yet, make a template with tracing paper of the exact size (sometimes the measure is not perfectly square). The glass should fit tightly. Once set in place the glass-top table is ready for use. You can protect the outer paper with a coat of varnish, but if you use vinyl covering this really isn't necessary.

# art deco table

# art deco table

Art Deco is a design style that was popular in the early part of the twentieth century. Its influence was evident in furniture, clothing and architecture as well as in illustration. As with many styles from the past, Art Deco designs resurface periodically with as much appeal as when they were at the height of popularity. Although this style is several decades old, many Art Deco designs are remarkably contemporary. Dark, subtle colors, sleek lines and shiny enamel come to mind when we think of Art Deco. These elements combine perfectly with the clean, simple lines of the parson's table.

The only time-consuming part of this project is the painting. To achieve the color used here you need enamel paint which takes a long time to dry, and at least three coats are essential. Since the painted surface is so prominent it is important to do a good job. The decorating time itself is short. We used Mystik aluminum tape for the silver stripes.

If you find an appropriate color in spray paint the project will go more quickly and you'll still have the high gloss finish called for here. The idea is to end up with a crisp, shiny, sleek table. Therefore, the paint you use is important.

The materials needed are: an 18-inch parson's table; paint sealer; wine-colored high gloss enamel paint; a 2-inch paint brush; paint thinner; sandpaper; 0000 steel wool; a roll of Mystik aluminum tape; a razor blade; a metal straightedge.

If you're not using spray paint, choose the color you want from swatches at the paint store and have it mixed. Prepare the table by sanding it until it is smooth all over. Pour some of the paint into the white sealer and mix it well. Usually a paint store puts a stick into the bag when you buy paint. Be sure to get one. Apply a primer coat of paint to all exposed areas of the table and let this dry overnight. Particles in the paint will make the finish feel bumpy and the table should be sanded smooth again. The better the surface the easier it will be to get a good-looking painted finish.

Before painting with the enamel spread newspapers around on the floor. Painting with enamel is not the same as painting with water base paint. You can't just slap it on. Each

coat should be applied as a thin, uniform layer so that the table will be evenly coated. Dip the brush into the paint and remove the excess on the rim of the can as you draw it out. Start at the center of the table so that the paint thins as you draw your brush to the outer edges. Coat the paint on in one direction across the table. Then feather it by gently stroking across the painted surface in the other direction. This is done with the very tip of the brush. Paint the sides and legs in the same way. Check to see that there are no drips where you may have used too much paint. There should be no buildup at the edges.

If you apply several thin coats of paint rather than one or two thick layers your table will be as smooth as glass. Do not touch it. Leave the table to dry for a full twenty-four hours. During the drying time dust will settle on the paint making the surface a little bumpy. Don't do anything about this while

Paint with high gloss enamel.

it is still tacky. Wait until the paint is absolutely dry to the touch.

Rub the surface with steel wool. This will dull the paint slightly but will help to eliminate the rough spots. Continue to apply more paint until the table is beautifully covered and looks even. There should be no streaks anywhere. Do not use steel wool on the final coat. You will have to live with the imperfections as it is more important for the finish to be glossy. At this point the tiny particles will hardly show. It helps to keep the table in an out-of-the-way place during the drying time.

The aluminum tape is about 2 inches wide. Leaving the paper backing on, slice it in various thicknesses with a straightedge and blade to get the different size bands. They should be cut longer than the actual measure, then trimmed at the end with the razor blade.

Use a straightedge to cut strips of aluminum tape.

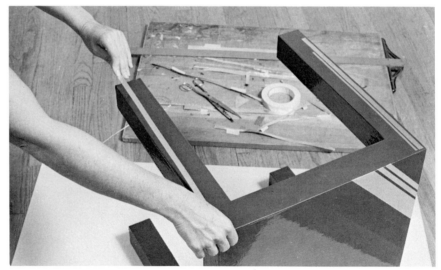

Line strip up so that it is straight before pressing in place.

The first wide strip can then be placed at a 45-degree angle across the top. To do this accurately, place a 45-degree triangle on the table. After that place the strips where they look attractive, using the edges of the table as a guide. Since the tape has a peel-away backing, you can try out the design before applying it permanently. The aluminum tape is extremely strong, so don't press it down until you know exactly where you want it. If you lift it the paint might come up with it. When ready, rub your finger over each strip to smooth it in place. You can add as much to the design as you want. I prefer to keep it simple.

Once you've taped the design, that's it. The table is ready to use.

# scalloped coffee table

The inspiration for this project came from the beautiful wall-covering and fabric designs of The Raintree Collection by Laura Ashley. This particular design lends itself to the cut-out border created here, but the project can be executed with any repeat border design that can be used both vertically and horizontally. Since this is a repeat pattern it can be cut to any width, but it looks best when kept to the same size as the front border of the table. In other words, the border around the top of the table is the same measure as the border around the sides.

This table is a long, low coffee table measuring 18 by 18 by 48 inches. Since it is a rather large piece of furniture meant for a prominent space, it is nice to keep the design subtle. I feel that the smaller parson's tables used as occasional tables can be more adventurous in design. In order for this project to work the background paint must be mixed to match the paper background perfectly. Also, the scallops must be cut out exactly since they will be displayed on a large area. Other than that there are no special warnings. The background color could be blue rather than creamy white but I felt that it would be easier to match the white—and that white would be more adaptable to other pieces in a room.

The paper for this project is heavy, soil-resistant vinyl. It's easy to work with and is best applied with Elmer's Glue-All. I found that it soaked up the glue and I needed quite a bit, so have enough on hand when you begin.

The materials needed are: a parson's table; a roll of Laura Ashley paper (this is the smallest amount that you can order); cuticle scissors; Elmer's Glue-All; fine black sandpaper such as 400; acrylic paint (beige—or mix raw umber with white); a 1-inch sponge brush; a razor blade; satin indoor wood varnish; a 2-inch varnish brush; paint thinner; 0000 steel wool; a rubber brayer (optional); a cloth or sponge; paste wax.

Mix the paint color so that it matches the background of your paper. For this project we used a drop of acrylic raw umber added to white latex paint. You will only need enough to cover the exposed area on the top of the table. For this paint job an inexpensive sponge brush is adequate. Brush the paint over the table in one direction and let it dry. If another coat is necessary apply it and again let it dry.

Since the paper is not as wide as the table, the border cannot be applied in one continuous strip. Cut enough pieces to form one long strip. Piece the strips together so that they

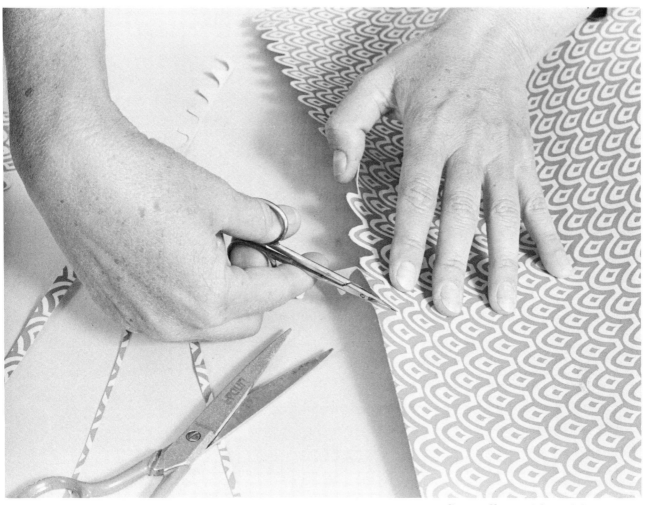

Cut scallops with cuticle scissors.

measure the length of your table and scallop. Next, measure the front edge of the table to determine how wide your border will be on the top of the table. Cut the strips for the top sides wide enough to fold over and cover the edges of the front and to tuck under the table for a neat, finished look. Do the same for the smaller pieces. When placed on the table the corners will not match up perfectly on the top so play around with them until they look best. The important thing is that the pattern match at the corners on the legs.

Apply each strip by coating the back of the paper with Elmer's glue. Do one at a time as the paper absorbs the glue quickly; if you apply the glue to all the strips at once they will dry. Use a wet sponge or sponge brush to dilute the glue as you spread it evenly over the paper. When the strips have been placed along the table top, roll a rubber brayer, rolling pin or similar object over them to be sure that they are secure. Excess glue may ooze out, easily removed by patting the

Mix paint to match background color of paper.

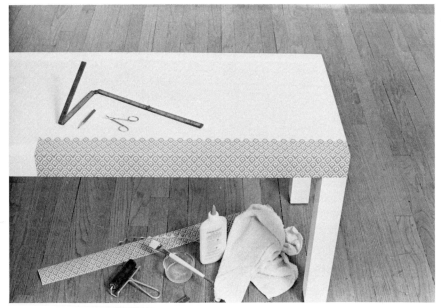

Match the paper so that the border is continuous.

edges with a damp sponge. Don't wipe it away as you may accidentally wrinkle or rip one of the scallops.

Crease the paper at the edge of the table and press the rest of it down on the front. This piece will extend below the front edge. Make a cut at the inside edge of each leg so that you can fold the paper in and under the table's edges. The top part of the legs will now be covered also.

Before going on, check all the glued pieces to be sure that there are no loose edges. Add a spot of glue where needed. Next cut out the strips to cover the legs. Be sure to cut the paper so that the pattern is going in the same direction as the other pieces. This is no time to reverse the pattern! Cut these

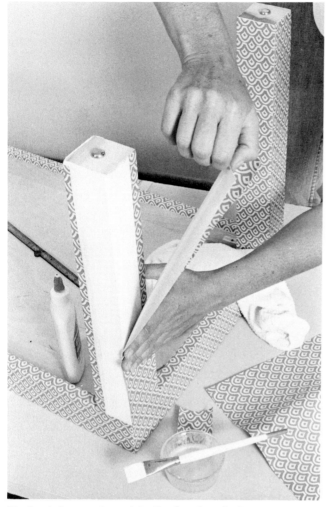

Each strip must match the border design.

Wipe away excess glue while mounting paper.

pieces wide enough to wrap around two sides of a leg, overlapping slightly on either side.

There is a lot of matching to be done here, so take your time. Not only are you matching the two pieces on each leg, you need to match the paper to the part of the leg that has already been covered. It's like doing a puzzle—and can be fun. Again, be sure to apply enough glue to the paper so that it is evenly coated before placing it on the leg. If there is any excess paper on the bottom or sides it can be trimmed with a razor blade after it has been glued in place.

Give the glue a few minutes to dry; it doesn't take long for it to create a bond between the paper and wood. If you have a staple gun the paper can be secured under the table. This is not necessary, just an added precaution.

Coat everything, including the under edges, with a satin finish indoor wood varnish. Apply this carefully. A thin coat is preferable to a thick layer. Varnish takes twenty-four

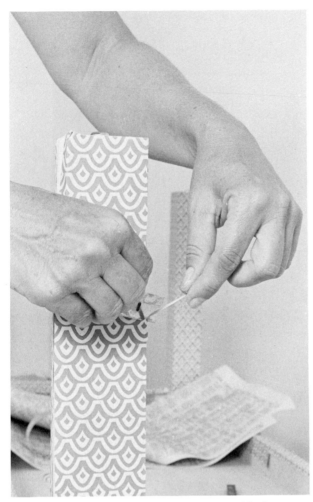

Trim excess paper with a sharp razor blade.　　Apply several coats of varnish over all.

hours to dry, therefore it is best to work in an area where the table can be left undisturbed. The satin finish is more appropriate for this project than a glossy finish.

With your brush full begin to spread the varnish from the center of the table to the outer edges. In this way the varnish will be thinnest at the edges of the table where drips are most likely to occur. Hold your brush very lightly and draw it over the surface in the opposite direction. Do not redip your brush in the varnish when doing this. Continue coating the rest of the table in the same way. Be careful to cover all areas with a thin coat. Varnishing is best done against the light so that you can see where you have applied it. Since it is clear it is often easy to miss spots.

Place your brush in a jar of paint thinner between applications to keep it soft and pliable. Three coats of varnish are usually sufficient, but you may want to do more. This will depend on how well the scalloped edges are covered. They

should feel fairly smooth to the touch and almost even with the table's surface. No matter how many coats of varnish you use, always let the previous coat dry completely before applying another.

When the final coat is dry, sand the table smooth with wet sandpaper. To do this, mix some soap suds in a cup of water. Douse the sandpaper in the water, then sand the table. Keep the paper wet while going over the entire surface. Wipe away all the grit with a cloth. Then rub everywhere with fine steel wool. Wipe away the particles. The table should feel very smooth.

For the final, sparkling touch, coat the table with a thin layer of furniture paste wax, such as Butcher's or Johnson's. Let it stand for ten minutes, then buff with a clean cloth. This will give your piece a fine patina and protective coating. You can place anything on the table now, even a wet drink, without marring the finish.

# suede and tile table

This cube table was created by accident. As it turned out, the effect is exactly what I wanted—an occasional cocktail table that blends with my carpet.

We were browsing in a tile shop and discovered beautiful 8-inch tiles that were placed in a square of four to form a design. Tile and carpet companies often display these sets of four mounted on a card which the manufacturer supplies. Once the tile design is discontinued the display card is no longer needed. While talking to the store owner about this project we found this was the case, and he offered us the tiles. They fit together perfectly on top of a 16-inch cube. By coincidence the rust- and sand-colored pattern is identical to the suede cloth that we had already acquired for the suede parson's table project described earlier.

If you are planning to do this project I suggest looking around for a tile pattern that accentuates the colors in your room. There is a wide variety to choose from and the tiles are not so expensive that you must settle for only discards. Our rug is sand-colored so I decided to use sand-colored suede for the effect I was seeking.

Suede cloth is marvelous for this project. The material doesn't ravel when cut, so the edges do not have to be folded or hemmed. This eliminates bulky edges at top and side seams. Remember this when choosing your fabric. Felt would work well also. Suede is easy to apply and transforms the cube into a soft upholstered piece of furniture. An alternative to matching your carpet color might be to match a fabric already in the room. Select the tiles and fabric at the same time to avoid a horrible mismatch.

This project can be done quickly and costs very little. You will need: one 16-inch wooden cube; enough fabric to completely cover four sides; a ruler or straightedge; a razor blade; Spra-Ment adhesive; four 8-inch tiles; tile adhesive; Scotchgard fabric protector (optional) to protect the fabric from soiling.

To begin, sand the wooden cube so that all exposed surfaces are absolutely smooth. If there are any gouges, cracks or unevenly matched edges or corners, fill them with wood putty. Borden's wood filler is excellent because it has a water base; it dries quickly and is easy to clean up. Apply it with a small putty knife. Be sure to let the wood filler dry thoroughly, then sand all areas smooth with medium grit sandpaper (320).

When applied to the cube, the fabric should cover the edge of the tiles. Therefore, the tiles are adhered before the fabric. If they do not fit exactly on top of the cube (some cubes are a bit irregular), plan to fill in the uneven areas around the edges with wood filler once the tiles have been secured. Tile

adhesive is available where tiles are sold or in most hardware stores. Apply it to the top of the cube with a putty knife. Set the tiles in place, butting them together so that the design fits perfectly. Let the tile adhesive dry before adjusting any areas that need wood filler. Sand any bumpy areas around the tiles.

Measure around the four sides of the cube (sometimes a 16-inch cube is not perfectly matched on all sides). Add a couple of inches to this measure for enough fabric to overlap the end seam, then cut one continuous piece. Measure from top to bottom and add 2 inches so that the fabric can be tucked under and glued or stapled to the inside of the cube for a finished look.

Using a straightedge and razor blade, cut out the rectangle that you have drawn to the exact measure on your fabric. Turn the fabric face down and liberally spray the back with Spra-Ment. If you prefer to use a white glue it should be thinned with water and brushed onto all exposed sides of the cube. However, for ease of handling and application without glue absorption by the fabric, I recommend Spra-Ment.

Line the fabric up flush with the top edge of the tiles. Press the side edge of the fabric down so that it is straight up and down on the cube. Using Spra-Ment lets you take the fabric up and put it down again if you don't get it straight the first time. While holding the fabric down with one hand pull it taut with the other so that it wraps around the cube and fits like skin. A wallpaper brush can be very handy for smoothing out wrinkles as you apply the fabric. As a substitute try a rolling pin. It is crucial that the top edge line up perfectly with the top of the tiles. If it is a bit higher it can be trimmed later, but it should not be lower as it will look uneven—and pretty awful.

Turn the cube on its side and stretch the fabric down and under the bottom to finish the outer covering. Check all sides to be sure the edges are glued securely. If not, add a drop of glue with your finger where needed. Once you are sure that the fabric is smooth on all four sides, staple it to the bottom inside of the cube.

To protect the fabric from soiling when in use you might want to give it a spray coating of Scotchgard. Some fabrics are mill-treated, and won't need another treatment. If this is the case, it will usually say so on the edge of the fabric. And there you have it—a stunning table for about fifteen dollars!

# painted rocking chair

# painted rocking chair

Painting is probably the most traditional way to finish raw furniture. In fact, the most common way to describe this furniture is to call it "unpainted," indicating that you must paint it in order to finish it. Sometimes a project is simply painted one color; at other times a piece may be painted in multicolors, such as painting each drawer of a dresser differently. More ornate furniture with raised areas is often painted quite elaborately according to the taste and talent of the craftworker.

Acrylic paint is used to decorate this child's rocker. It comes in tubes or jars and is available in an endless variety of colors. If you'd like to buy a set of small tubes for just one project, Grumbacher puts out sets of various sizes. Or you can buy tubes of the individual colors that you need.

A child's wooden rocker is a common item and seems to be readily available where unfinished furniture is sold. If you already have a rocker you'd like to use, the old finish should first be removed. With a fairly old chair, chances are this finish is shellac. It can be removed by first soaking a rag with denatured alcohol and rubbing it over the chair. Then sand with heavy sandpaper. This will take some care in removing the finish around the rungs. If the chair is painted and in good condition, you might be able to sand it smooth and repaint right over the old finish. If not in good condition, remove the paint as with the shellac, substituting paint remover for alcohol. Sand the surface before repainting.

The design shown here fits nicely on this size rocker. The curled-up cat could also be painted onto a stool or perhaps a

headboard. Any illustration can be used. If you have a favorite illustration, use the grid method to copy and scale it to size. Simply trace it and draw squares over the picture. Then make a larger grid and copy the design square by square. Transfer the design by rubbing the back with pencil and tracing over the front of the outline with a pen. This will create a pencil outline on the chair.

Once you have traced and transferred the design to the rocker, outline the design by painting it with black acrylic.

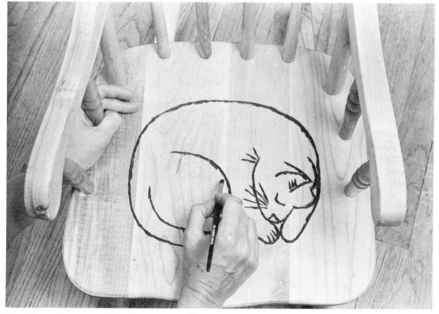

Transfer design onto rocker.

Outline design with black acrylic paint.

Use a small, soft artist's brush for this. As you can see by the photograph, the outline is not perfectly accurate. It is not necessary to be precise. In fact, this is part of the charm.

Next mix your colors. We wanted delicious, delicate colors; the pastel shades of sherbet seemed perfect. When mixing your colors, be sure that they go together. Keep them the same value. For example, bright red, purple, blue, and green are of the same intensity, which makes them harmonious. A piece of cardboard or waxed paper on a board makes a good palette for mixing. We used little paper cups available in a

Fill in with color.

five-and-ten or variety store. A palette knife is also useful.

To achieve the colors used here the following basic paints are mixed with white (always go lighter than you think you should, using just a little color in the white): napthol or Grumbacher red for pink; napthol red with slightly more ultramarine blue for lavender; chrome oxide green and cadmium yellow for green; cadmium yellow and raw sienna for yellow. Cadmium orange and white are mixed for the cat and the seat is a mixture of cobalt blue and white. All the basic colors can be added to white for a paler pastel shade. Be sure to mix your paints thoroughly before using them.

Once the designs are outlined in black and you have mixed your colors, you can begin to fill in the different areas. Begin with the pale orange cat, then add his darker orange stripes. (Use the same mixture, adding more orange.) Once the cat has been painted, fill in the seat area around it with pale blue. Each chair rung is a different color as are the arms and legs.

Each square equals 1 inch.

This project takes a bit of patience, but it is not difficult. Jon did the work on the rocker and found that with good background music the painting made for a relaxing afternoon.

Let the paint dry thoroughly once you have finished. Since this is water base paint, it won't take long. The paint is delicate, however, and since the color is so light, the chair should be handled carefully and put in an out-of-the-way place to dry. Once dry spray the entire chair, front, back and around the rungs, with Krylon spray varnish. Do not stand too close to the chair when spraying. You should apply a fine, misty coating to avoid drips forming where too much varnish has been sprayed. Let this coat dry and reapply. Five or six coats should make this rocker durable enough for any child's use.

# hearts and ticking dresser

# hearts and ticking dresser

Fabric-covered furniture is not new, but it is looking better and better all the time. This is due to the wide variety of decorator fabrics now available and the improved products for applying them. I am especially fond of red and white ticking and since it is so easy to find, I thought it might be fun to use for a young-looking dresser. While I used a staple gun for reinforcement here and there, it really wasn't necessary as the fabric adhesive was so effective and easy to use.

This design idea works best on a five-drawer dresser. The hearts are stenciled right over the fabric, and is easy to do with the right materials. The stencilboard is available in art supply stores. With the added application of the stencil design you can turn an ordinary object into a bright, bold piece.

For a variation of the idea you could cover each drawer with a different fabric. Sticking to the red and white theme, calico, checks, stripes, or tiny prints could be combined for a striking, busy look. When materials all vary but relate in the size of the prints, the effect can be eye-catching. Curtains, bedspread and accessories can be fun to make in corresponding fabrics. The director's chair was an afterthought, but since the stencil was already made, it was easy enough to carry the heart design further. All kinds of objects could be decorated in this theme.

On an otherwise dull or rainy day keeping you indoors, this project is guaranteed to cheer you. It can be completed by the end of the day.

Materials needed are: three to four yards of fabric depending on the width; a five-drawer bureau; Spra-Ment adhesive; scissors; a ruler; a triangle, stencilboard, a stipple brush; red acrylic paint; a wallpaper brush (optional); a razor blade or X-acto knife.

Measure and cut out the large pieces of fabric first for the sides and top of the dresser. Remember to cut each piece so that the stripes run up and down. Cut the two long side strips with an extra inch to bring around to the front rim. Cut these side pieces long enough to come slightly over the top and under the bottom of the dresser. Next cut five pieces for the

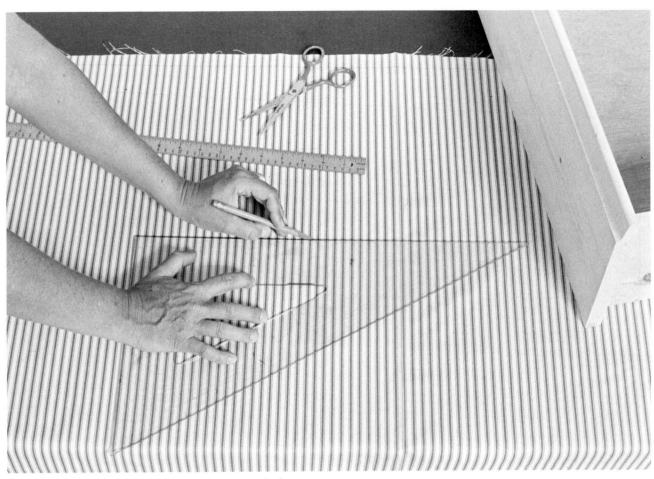

Accurately measure the pieces to cover each drawer.

drawer fronts. They should be large enough to allow the fabric to be stapled to the inside and bottom of each drawer, eliminating frayed edges. Then cut narrow strips for the areas exposed between the drawers, for the bottom of the dresser, and for the strip at the top.

Spread the large pieces out on newspaper and spray generously with Spra-Ment adhesive. Line the fabric up at the top edge of the dresser and press it firmly all the way down the back edge to the bottom of the dresser. If you have enough width, leave a little fabric overlapping at the back. Next smooth the top edge over the top rim of the bureau so that the stripes are straight. Check to be sure that they aren't wiggly.

At this point a wallpaper brush comes in handy. Found in wallpaper and paint stores, this stiff, wooden-handled bristle

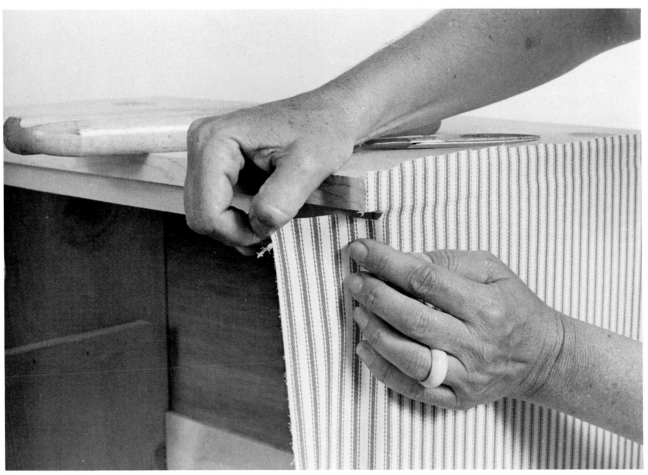

Leave extra fabric to overlap onto front edge.

brush smooths the covering while removing air bubbles trapped underneath. If you don't have one, smooth the fabric as best you can with your hand. Hold the loose edge taut with one hand and smooth with the other as you attach the fabric to the side of the bureau. When both sides are covered, spray and place the top piece so that it fits perfectly at the sides (the stripes here run front to back). If there is a little extra fabric it can be trimmed with a razor blade. Smooth the fabric and pull the front edge down over the front edge of the bureau. Tuck this under the lip and be sure to smooth and secure it.

The stripes on the drawers should line up with the stripes that are coming down from the top of the bureau. Spray the back of each piece and lay it on the drawer front. It is easiest to do this with the drawers removed and placed on a table.

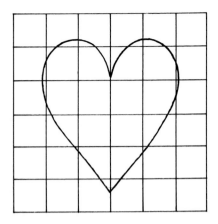

Transfer heart outlines to stencil board.

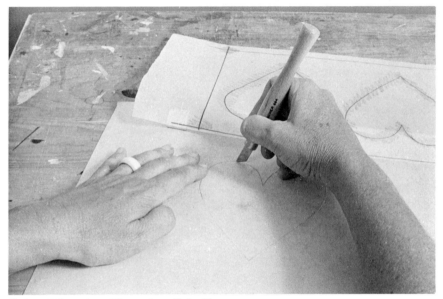

Cut out hearts with a stencil knife.

Pull the fabric over the front edges so that they fit very tautly. The fabric adhesive makes it possible to pull up and replace a piece if it is not perfect the first time. Adjust the fabric as you apply it. Press the material over the top of the drawer and down onto the inside. Do the same on the bottom. Each drawer should match the one above it.

Last, cover the small strips of wood that are left and check to be sure that all the fabric is secure. If you have to do a touch up, squirt a little of the adhesive on your finger and apply it where needed. This can be removed from your hands with paint thinner or nail polish remover.

A stipple brush is used to apply acrylic paint to the fabric.

To make the stencil, cut a strip of stencilboard the exact size of the drawer front. Trace the heart and transfer it to the stencil so that you have five evenly spaced hearts in a row. Using a razor blade or X-acto knife cut out the heart shapes. The reason for making a stencil with five hearts rather than using one heart repeatedly is that it is important for them to be perfectly lined up. This is a graphic design that depends on accuracy for part of its appeal.

Tape the stencil to the first drawer. Squirt a small amount of acrylic paint into a shallow dish (we used Grumbacher red). Dip a medium-sized stipple brush into the paint and tap the

color onto the fabric. (You will probably need two coats as this must be done without overloading the brush with paint.) With each successive drawer, stencil one less heart. When the first coat has dried, reapply the paint to all the hearts if you feel it is necessary.

The director's chair is done the same way. Remove the back piece of canvas and stencil the hearts with white acrylic paint. If you want to add a protective coating to the fabric it can be sprayed with 3M Scotchgard.

Once I began applying hearts to the furniture I wanted to continue and it took great restraint to keep hearts off the walls. However, for an added touch you might want to stencil the window shades.

# paper patchwork blanket chest

# paper patchwork blanket chest

Patchwork quilts have become so popular in recent years that their design influence can be seen in many other areas. Stenciled floors and furniture have borrowed these traditional patterns and even fabric for clothing has been printed to resemble patchwork. We thought that wallpaper patchwork would lend itself to an interesting project that could be expanded beyond the furniture piece to include floors, a chair, maybe even a wall. I enjoyed working on this chest, but I must admit that it is not a project that can be done in a day—and a wall or floor would take a very long time.

Almost every print, large or small, in any color, can be used. At first I thought that the brighter colors of shocking pink and green would be unsuitable for the overall feeling, but when I tried them, they looked quite pleasing. Actually, the pink pieces made the piece bright and more interesting than if I had left them out.

It is not difficult to obtain all the wallpaper you need. As wallpaper designs are discontinued the sample books become obsolete; they're perfect sources for this project. Wallpaper, hardware and paint stores usually throw them away if they are not used. Many nursery schools, art students and craft-workers have made requests for them and most stores hold onto the books until they run out of space. Go into several stores and ask for their old sample books. If you can acquire two or three you will have enough variety to do any project with patchwork pieces. You can use either of the diagrams that are offered or combine the two as I have done.

The diamond shapes that make up the patchwork effect here are two different sizes. They both form motifs familiar from traditional American folk art. The larger diamond forms a box shape when grouped together in a set of three. The narrower diamond forms a starburst effect. As you can see, both designs are based on circles.

The materials needed are: a variety of wallpaper sheets; Elmer's Glue-All; a 1-inch sponge brush; a shallow bowl; an X-acto knife; a metal straightedge; tracing paper; a pencil; tape; varnish; a varnish brush; paint thinner; a sponge; a rubber brayer (optional).

Begin by tracing the diamond diagrams on separate pieces of tracing paper. Trace the design, then turn your tracing over and trace the diagram again so that you end up with a complete star. Do this for both patterns. The two stars will serve as your master templates. Don't cut them up! Make tracings of each.

Tape the tracings to a stack of about six pieces of wallpaper, chosen so that they vary in design and color. Cut them out with a straightedge and sharp blade in the X-acto knife. This will yield forty-eight small diamonds and thirty-six large

Star pattern

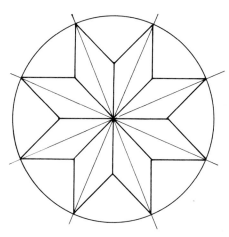

Box pattern

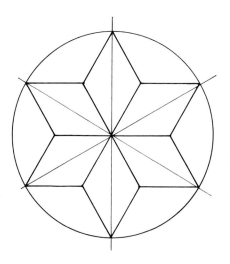

ones. Each time you need more diamonds you will have to trace the diagram from the master template. A large project, such as this, will take hundreds of diamonds. Cut out a whole batch before beginning. Accuracy is extremely important since the fit of the diamonds depends on it. However, patchwork designs are extremely forgiving. An error now and then can hardly be seen in the overall scheme.

This chest is a good shape for the patchwork design. You might consider a desk, a small cabinet, or even a cube as well. Sand the raw wood so that you have a smooth surface to work on. I primed the wood first with a coat of latex paint. If you paint the wood first, or apply a coat of shellac, it will be easier to glue the paper down.

Cutting design through six pieces of wallpaper.

Pour about a quarter of the large bottle of Elmer's glue into a shallow bowl and add a small amount of water. Mix thoroughly. Don't dilute the glue a lot, just enough to thin it so that it spreads easily. A 1-inch sponge brush is used to apply the glue to the bench.

Find the center of the piece by drawing an "X" between diagonal corners, then draw a pencil line across the middle so that you have a guide for lining up the first group of diamonds. When beginning to place the paper pieces it will be helpful to keep referring to the designs. I found that sometimes I forgot the pattern because the designs of the wallpaper were so distracting. The starburst is easier to follow than the box design.

Star pattern partially completed.

Spread the glue on a small area in the center of the piece to be covered. Place the first diamond at the center on the penciled line and continue. You're on your way. As you place the diamonds one after the other you will start to select pieces that seem to fit best in color and pattern. No planning went into this beforehand. It was done strictly at random. At one point I felt that I should have planned it out, but quickly realized how impossible that would have been. The design simply evolves as you add more and more pieces. Stand back occasionally to view the overall effect—too hard to do with your nose practically in the glue pot. Keep a wet sponge handy at all times. You'll need it. Use the rubber brayer from time to time to roll over a finished area.

Once the entire front is covered with one pattern, go on to the top using the box pattern. Start this in the same way. Find the center and create a box. As I mentioned before, this is a bit trickier than the star so refer to the basic pattern shown here. When I was halfway through I realized that no two pieces ever go in the same direction. Therefore, if you suddenly find that two diamonds are up and down right next to one another, the pattern is wrong. These pieces are larger and you might select each color and pattern more carefully than for the star pattern. The boxes should be immediately apparent. Continue the box design up the back, or you can switch back to the star. I used the star pattern on the sides.

A rubber brayer is used to roll over and secure paper pieces.

No two pieces of the box pattern are placed in the same direction.

Once the chest is covered apply a coat of polyurethane over all.

Once all the exposed areas are covered with patchwork, check to be sure that all edges are glued down. If there are some areas that need attention, now is the time to add glue. When the glue has dried, coat the entire piece with polyurethane varnish in a glossy or satin finish, whichever you prefer. I like the shiny effect, but the satin finish will make the piece look more authentic. Brush over all areas, put the bench out of the mainstream, and let it dry overnight. Two or three coats should be applied before rubbing the surface with fine steel wool if it needs smoothing. This finish is very tough and the paper pieces will be completely protected. One of these days I am going to cover a floor. It would be so much fun to walk on, but first I have to be darn sure that I will love it forever. It is permanent.

**metal tile planter**

# metal tile planter

I may go on repeating myself throughout this book, but every time I work on a cube I get excited by the results. Cubes are so versatile. This time I needed a plant holder, so the cube was turned upside-down. This project is made with the basic 16-inch cube, but you need to add to it to make it larger. What this project actually calls for is a 17-inch cube which is impossible to come by unless you have it made. A lumberyard will comply or you might ask where cubes are sold. Some shops will make one to order and the price is not much more than the cost of the basic size.

The reason for the larger size is so that you can use inexpensive stove tiles for the covering and they only come in 4¼-inch size. Those used here are brushed aluminum Metalco tiles. They come in copper as well. By adding wood to the sides of a 16-inch cube you create a double thickness around the edge, giving you a thick border and making the cube look quite substantial. To make the planter sturdy enough to be placed outdoors the tiles can be used on most of the inside and on the bottom so that the wood is covered.

The most time-consuming part of this project is remaking the cube. Applying the tiles can be done in a matter of minutes. They come in a box with pressure-sensitive tabs that stick to the back of the tiles as well as the surface of the wood. For the top edge we used Mystik aluminum tape.

The materials needed for this project are: one 16-inch cube; 64 brushed aluminum stove tiles; a roll of Mystik aluminum tape; Elmer's glue; sandpaper or electric sander; a hammer; nails; five pieces of composition board (four 16½ by 16½-

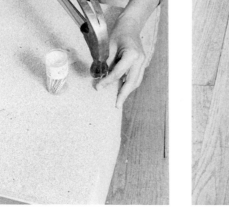

inch pieces for the sides and one 17 by 17-inch piece for the bottom); a wood plane; enamel spray paint if you want to paint the inside.

The boards can be cut in a lumberyard, but if you can cut the wood yourself, by all means do so. Begin by putting Elmer's Glue-All along the edges of the sides of the cubes. Line up one edge of a piece of composition board with the edge of the cube so that it is flush with the bottom. This board will overlap one inch on one side. Hammer small nails into the board every few inches to attach it to the cube. Fasten each side in this way. As I've mentioned before, these unfinished cubes are not always a perfect measure, therefore you may

Plane down the sides so that they are even.

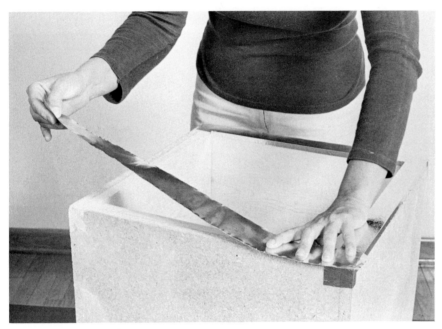

Cover edges with self-adhesive aluminum tape.

have some excess on the top. This can be trimmed, but it is important that the bottom fit well so that you won't have a wobbly planter. Turn the cube over and secure the bottom piece the same way as the sides. This 17-inch board should fit perfectly on all edges. Turn the cube right side up and trim any uneven areas with a wood plane. Fill any cracks or uneven areas with wood putty; let it dry, then sand.

Cut a piece of aluminum tape a little larger than 17 inches. Press one edge down firmly on the corner of the cube and smooth the strip across the top of one side. This tape is 2 inches wide and will overlap on either side. To be sure that it is smooth run a roller or similar object over the strip.

Cover outside with stove tiles.

Continue to do this on all top edges, overlapping the tape at each corner.

Lay a metal ruler or straightedge across the corner so that it makes a diagonal line from the outer corner edge to the inside corner edge. With a sharp razor blade make a straight cut. This will create a mitered corner. Peel away the excess piece of aluminum tape and the corner will butt together.

The small tabs for adhering the tiles come in a package with the box of tiles. Peel them off and place them on the back corners of the tiles. When placing each tile on the planter it is extremely important to be exact. You don't get two chances with this tape. If the tile is crooked you have to remove it and the tape will not work a second time. In that case, the tape must be peeled off (not easy) and new tabs used. If you try to stick a tile back in place with the old tabs, it will fall off the planter. So try to get it right the first time.

One more note of caution: If there has been the slightest error in calculation when making this cube, you may find that the tiles will not butt together to cover the cube completely. It might be a good idea to begin by placing the cube on its side and laying the tiles in place before gluing. If they are slightly off, cover yourself by spraying the entire cube with silver paint. In this way a slight gap between the tiles will not be noticeable.

Line up the first row of tiles with the top of the cube. (It is best to start at the top and work down.) Press each tile firmly against the cube with the palm of your hand. In no time the entire cube will be covered. If you want to continue on the inside do so, or you might want to spray paint it. If you do, cover the top edge with paper so that the paint won't get on the silver edge. The interior sides of our cube are covered with aluminum tape. The inside bottom is covered with aluminum tiles. They do not fit over the entire bottom, but enough of the area is covered to hold a potted plant. The exposed areas on the inside bottom are covered with more aluminum tape. The bottom of the planter should be covered as well if the planter is to be used outside. If not, this is not necessary.

# ivy plant stand

# ivy plant stand

Plants have become so popular for home decoration that almost everyone has a green thumb or has acquired one out of necessity. Even greenhouses are becoming household additions and the smallest apartments often display a variety of indoor plants in window greenhouses. Growing plants in offices with no natural light has become possible with the introduction of special grow lights.

To house all these plants we need holders, stands, and hanging pots, and it's fun to search for various shapes and sizes. Containers have become a main part of our decorating schemes. The small wooden plant stand that I decorated here is quite inexpensive and can be found along with other unfinished furniture. A paper cutout climbing vine seemed perfect for the spool base.

It is difficult to find one long vine that is the exact size for the object; a variety of leaves of similar colors will work as well. A small inexpensive book of leaves (easy to find in a bookstore) is best for this project. If you take your design elements from one source the weight of the paper and the printing quality will be consistent.

First sand the table and give it a coat of shellac thinned with denatured alcohol. If you prefer, a primer coat of paint can be applied to seal the wood. Do not put too much on as it will form drip marks down the spool. For this project it is easiest to use enamel spray paint in any color. I used white because the decoration is green with touches of red berries and purple flowers which show up best against a white background. It will also look well with a similarly decorated director's chair. The chair I used was completely white, and I wrapped green vines around the legs and arms. Once varnished, the chalky white color mellows to antique ivory.

Materials needed for this project include: the wooden plant stand; latex or enamel paint; a brush (if not using spray paint); designs to be cut out; cuticle scissors; Elmer's Glue-All; a sponge; sandpaper; spray varnish; antiquing mix (optional); and green acrylic paint if you want to add a border of green paint around the top of the table edge.

The plant stand should be given sufficient coats of paint to completely cover it so that no wood grain shows through. Each coat must be sanded after drying thoroughly. When using a base of white paint, two or three coats are usually required. For a darker shade one coat is often enough. It is not as easy to paint a curved item as a flat piece of furniture. Coat the entire surface, including the underside of the top. This will seal it and keep moisture from lifting the paint away from the wood if it gets wet or is used in a greenhouse.

Select the design elements carefully and be sure that you have enough to extend from one end of the planter to the other. Cuticle scissors are the easiest to handle for a very neat cutting job; they enable you to cut around curved areas and to remove the tiny bits of paper between leaves and stems.

Cuticle scissors are best for cutting out delicate designs.

The more accurately you cut, the better-looking your piece will be.

Spread the cut-out leaves on your work surface so that you can arrange them. They should appear to wind around the spool as naturally as possible. Once the basic design is established you can add small flowers or berries for interest. A butterfly is always good to have for color as well as filler in a space that might have been missed. Greeting cards are good sources of butterflies and similar objects. Very good paperback books are also available on almost any subject; they're worth purchasing for the birds, butterflies, leaves, and so on used in decoupage. Craft shops also carry packaged prints that are quite lovely. However, when doing a project larger than a small box, it is more economical to purchase a book.

Once the design is cut out, glue each piece in place on the planter with Elmer's glue. Squirt a small amount on the back of each cutout and place it where you have planned. Pat it with a slightly damp sponge to secure it as well as to remove any excess glue that may ooze out at the edges. Be sure that each cutout is glued down firmly.

Wash your hands from time to time to avoid getting glue on the front of a leaf while pressing it in place. If this happens your fingers may stick to the cutout and pull away some of the printing. When the vine is complete add a few more cutouts to the base of the planter. Choose another design to cut out for the top of the table. You can cut apart a bunch of flowers

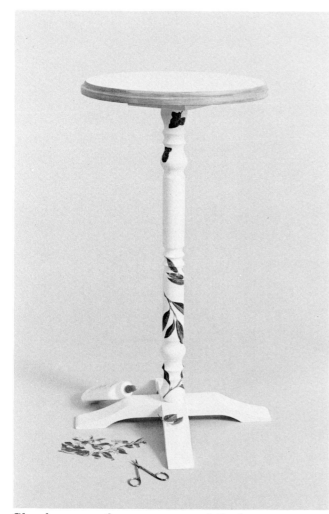

Glue leaves so they wrap around the base.

Arrange cutouts to create a border design.

to create a design to go completely around the top. Space the pieces generously, then fill in where needed with a few more leaves and buds.

Stand back and look over all sides. If more cutouts are needed, add them now before varnishing. Then apply Krylon spray varnish on all exposed areas, including the underside, to seal the painted surface. This varnish dries in about an hour when another coating can be applied. This will give the planter a very glossy finish. You can continue to spray many coats of varnish, letting each dry before applying another. Since I prefer a satin finish, after two spray coats I began applying regular satin finish varnish with a varnish brush. If you don't want to invest in both varnishes, either one is fine from start to finish. The spray varnish is much thinner and will therefore require more coats. Since it dries quickly this is no problem. The varnish that comes in a can must be left to dry for twenty-four hours; however, three coats will cover sufficiently.

Once varnished the plant stand is delicately antiqued.

Antiquing this piece is optional, but the effect is rather nice and enhances the design. It creates a smoky look and softens the color. The antiquing mixture can be purchased in an art supply or hobby shop or you might like to make your own. The best that I have found is a mix of equal parts boiled linseed oil, mineral spirits or paint thinner and oil-base raw umber. A small amount will go a long way, so buy the materials in small quantities. An easier way to achieve the antiquing, but not quite as nice, is with a small amount of acrylic raw umber diluted slightly with water.

Using a small (¼-inch) brush, liberally cover one section of the planter at a time. Yes, right over the design and all. Then, with a clean rag, wipe away the excess leaving a trace of the antiquing around the edges of the design as well as the planter. Let the mixture collect around the crevices and base of the planter. When in doubt as to the amount always remove more rather than less. The finish should appear to be slightly shaded; the best antiquing job is very subtle. Once done, do not touch the planter for twenty-four hours if the mixture has an oil base, one or two hours for acrylic or water base. When dry, seal it with another coat of varnish. Again, let the varnish dry overnight.

Slightly wet a piece of 400 black WetorDry sandpaper and gently rub it over the entire surface. Use a light touch. The purpose is merely to smooth the surface and to remove any

Protect finish with several coats of spray varnish.

particles that may have settled on the varnish while drying. Wipe away the sand grit and for an even smoother finish go over the piece with fine 0000 steel wool. The design will be slightly raised from the surface, giving it a three-dimensional look. This is more interesting than a design that is completely submerged under many many coats of varnish.

For the finale, apply a coat of furniture paste wax, such as Butcher's or Johnson's, let it stand for ten minutes, then buff with a soft cloth. The finish will absolutely shine.

# modular storage cubes

# modular storage cubes

Wooden storage cubes are easy to obtain and can be purchased in varying sizes. They are marvelous for all kinds of uses as we have demonstrated. While the cubes shown so far have been used singly, they can certainly be grouped together to expand the possible uses. Two or three placed together and topped with cushions take up little space as a seating unit. And they have the added advantage of doubling as storage units. They can be placed on the floor as we have, hung on a wall, or stacked one on top of the other.

The idea behind this project is to take advantage of predetermined patterns. This is not the same as repeating one pattern. The exciting thing about modular designs such as these is that no matter how you place the different surfaces, they always go together. The pattern usually looks a lot more complicated than it actually is. Jon Aron is a graphic designer as well as a photographer. He designed these cubes so that they could be duplicated by anyone. This project is not difficult, but it does require patience.

The cubes used for this are made of composition board. They are smooth and sturdy and won't warp. The sides are perfect squares and the pattern is made by dividing each square into four smaller squares. The design rule here is: Whatever you draw must either start or stop at an end or in the middle of a side. With this rule, whatever pattern you create on one side will join with the pattern on the next cube or on the adjacent side of the same cube. These geometric designs are dramatic when complete. If you feel confident enough to create your own, you can follow our painting techniques; if not, use Jon's design as is, or choose other color combinations.

The materials needed are: two or more storage cubes that are smooth and free of defects; white primer paint; white spray paint; Krylon spray paint in leather brown, icy grape, regal blue and banner red; masking tape; newspapers; a pushpin; stencilboard; Spra-Ment; spray varnish; Mars black acrylic paint; a 2-inch paint brush; a razor blade.

Begin by applying a coat of primer to the outside of the

At the halfway mark draw a line across the center of each side.

cubes. It may take three coats with light sanding in between to get a smooth surface. Keeping the cubes smooth is important for this project. When well-covered and smooth, spray the outside of all sides with white paint. This will give the painted surface a bright glossy finish.

The designs on these cubes are made from three elements: squares, half-circles and quarter-circles. The squares are created by measuring the halfway mark and drawing a line across the center of each side, making sure everything lines up on both cubes. Next mask off the square to be painted by pressing masking tape firmly on the penciled lines around the square. The sides of the cube touching this square are covered with newspaper taped to the edge. To mask off the rest of the top surface cut a piece of stencilboard 20 by 20 inches. From this board cut a square out of one corner leaving a 1-inch margin. The square should be about ⅜ inch larger than the area to be painted. This mask is used for all the squares.

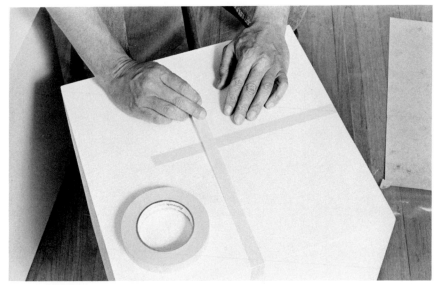

Place masking tape along the penciled lines.

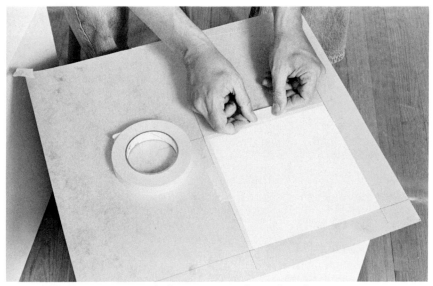

Mask off all areas around the square to be painted.

Spray one square on each side of each cube.

Spray a light coat of Spra-Ment on the back of the mask. Place the mask on top of the cube and press it down. It will stick while you are spray painting and can later be removed. The adhesive will prevent the paint from getting under the stencil and will assure a clean line.

Spray one red square on each side of each cube. Let them dry. Then mask off the square diagonally opposite and spray it grape. You may want to stop right there. You will have a checkerboard effect when the cubes are placed together.

However, the design possibilities expand when you add the curved shapes and the unit becomes more interesting.

The curved masks are also cut from stencilboard. If the cubes are 18 inches you will need half-circle and quarter-circle masks with a 9-inch radius. To make the masks without

Make half-circle and quarter-circle masks with a 9-inch radius.

the aid of a giant compass, mark off 9 inches on a strip of cardboard. Put a pushpin in one end and poke a pencil through the other end of the 9-inch measure. Place the pushpin end of the cardboard strip into the stencilboard and using the pencil end swing it around making a perfect circle on the board. Cut this out and make another. Spray a light coating of adhesive to the back of each before pressing it on the cube.

There are five surfaces on a cube. Make a brown semicircle on two surfaces. On each of the other three surfaces place two blue quarter-circles in any position at all. The more variety, the better.

This combination of colors and designs is one of infinite variety. You can use the same masks to do a completely differ-

ent color scheme. What if you make a mistake? It can easily be corrected. Save the inside pieces of the half- and quarter-circle masks. By using the half-circle shape you can lay it over the brown semicircle. It will fit perfectly. Then spray the correct color needed to clean up a fuzzy edge or messy area.

Mix a small quantity of mars black acrylic paint with white latex indoor paint. This will make a medium gray for the inside of the cubes. When the cubes are completely dry, brush on a polyurethane finish inside and out. Two or three coats yield a shiny protective coating. Or use Krylon spray varnish and apply at least five coats. If you eliminate this last step the paint will get dirty and chipped with use. After all this work it is best to protect the cubes with varnish.

# basket weave dresser

Wallpaper isn't what it used to be. Almost any kind of design or feeling you want can be found in wallcovering—and not in just the expensive decorator lines either. This five-drawer dresser is a prime example. The bold, geometric basket weave pattern in chocolate brown and silver is handsome and readily available. Wallpaper is probably the simplest way to cover an unfinished bureau. You might want to use some leftover from a room you papered.

The important thing here is accuracy in matching the pattern from drawer to drawer and in duplicating the background color in paint. It was not necessary to have this brown mixed—we found it in regular latex house paint. I usually don't recommend latex for furniture as enamel is much more durable, but when given several coats of varnish it looks beautiful and is just as strong.

The paper used for this project is water-resistant Waltex vinyl wallcovering and so little is needed that it takes only the scraps from a wallpaper job. Of course if you aren't planning to cover the walls, you will have to buy a roll—the least you can order. In that case you might consider a paper that you can use elsewhere, perhaps the bathroom. For small amounts of paper, consider using Contact self-adhesive covering. The designs have been greatly expanded.

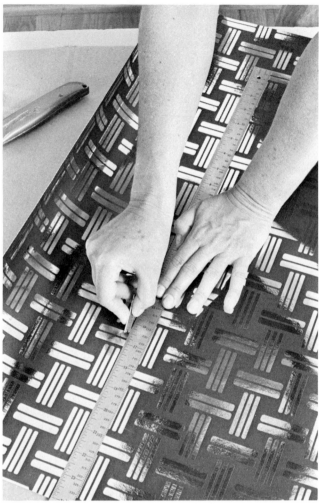

Measure and cut paper pieces for each drawer.

The materials needed are: a five-drawer dresser; dark brown latex paint; a 2-inch paint brush; glossy polyurethane varnish; paint thinner; Spra-Ment adhesive or Elmer's Glue-All; a razor blade or X-acto knife; a wallpaper brush (optional); sandpaper.

Sand the dresser smooth. Sometimes the edges on these unfinished bureaus are rather rough and can be rounded with a sanding block while sanding. If there are any gouges, cracks or imperfections, fill them with Borden's Professional Carpenter's Wood Filler. Let this dry before sanding.

Next paint the bureau. If you are using a white or pastel paint it is a good idea to use a coat of primer or sealer before applying the final coats. The dark brown covers in one application. Even though the front of the drawers will be covered, it's a good idea to paint them to be sure that the exposed areas are finished.

Measure the front of each drawer. Sometimes they are not perfectly matched. Cut each piece of wallpaper using a metal

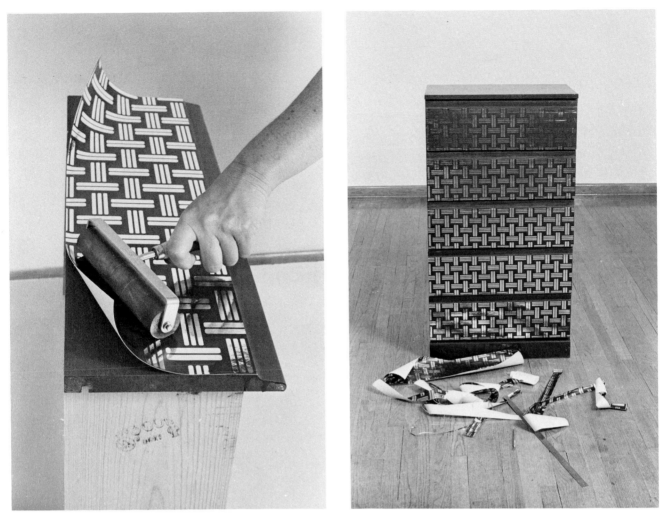

Press paper down firmly when mounting.

straightedge and a sharp blade. Be sure that each piece is identical so that the drawer being covered lines up with the one above it. The wallpaper can be applied one of two ways. If you use Spra-Ment adhesive, spray it over the back of the paper and onto the drawer front. Let this dry a bit so that the paper and the bureau drawer are tacky. Fuse the paper to the drawer. Line the paper up at one end of the drawer front and be sure to put it on straight. Continue until all the drawers are covered. A wallpaper brush or roller can be used to further smooth down the paper so that it is affixed on all edges. If you use Elmer's glue it should be spread evenly over the back of the paper.

Brush on the polyurethane varnish wherever the wood is exposed. Two or three thin coats are needed and each should dry overnight. Sand each coat lightly for a smooth finish. For an added touch, the inside of each drawer can be lined with the same wallpaper covering.

# burlap wine rack holder

There are many unusual and good looking wine holders on the market, but they are often very expensive. With so many people enjoying wine, a neat wine holder seems like a good project—especially since you can make it for around twelve dollars. This wine holder is made from a 14-inch wooden cube. It takes up little space in an apartment and can accommodate a commercially manufactured rack or one that you assemble yourself. If it's turned right side up it can hold an ice bucket for parties. And it is even attractive when you don't have the money to keep it filled with wine.

The burlap covering costs next to nothing and doesn't have to be seamed or finished in any way on the edges. The red paint and stencil lettering seem appropriate although another color matching your room could be used.

As if it weren't enough that this project looks good, takes up little space, and costs very little, it can be completed in less than an hour. So, if you're caught short the day before Christmas without a gift for someone on your list, this may turn out to be better than anything you could buy.

The materials needed are few: a 14-inch wooden cube; red acrylic paint; stencil letters; a stipple brush; a yard of burlap; Spra-Ment; scissors; Krylon flame red spray paint.

Apply coat of spray paint to inside of cube.

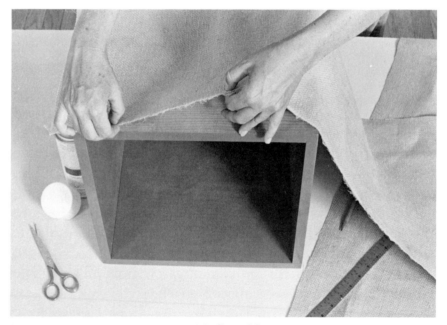

Spray one side of the burlap with Spra-Ment.

The inside of the cube and rim are painted first. Spray the inside with the red spray paint, let it dry and reapply. Paint the rim, letting the paint extend slightly onto the sides.

Cut the pieces of burlap large enough so that two sides of the cube can be covered at once. These pieces should also be large enough to overlap slightly onto sides three and four and tuck onto the back.

Coat one side of the first burlap piece with Spra-Ment adhesive. Place the finished edge of the fabric at the edge of the cube and wrap the burlap around so that it is taut.

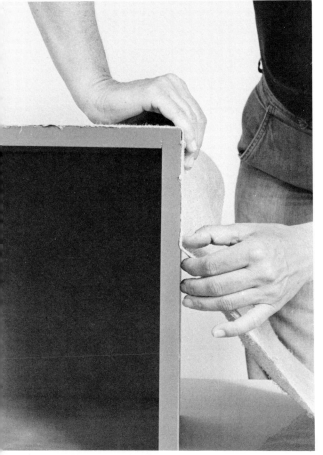

When wrapping burlap, line up with edge of cube.

Stencil letters diagonally across side of cube.

Smooth it down everywhere. Burlap sticks well with this adhesive.

Turn the cube over and apply the sticky burlap to the next side. Cut one piece to fit the back perfectly. Spray this piece and affix it to the back so that it covers the edges.

Turn the cube on its side and place a strip of masking tape across the cube so that you have a straight line for stenciling the letters. These letters come on one plastic stencil sheet and can be purchased in a five-and-ten or an art supply store. Squirt a little of the red acrylic paint into a shallow dish or on a piece of cardboard and dip the stipple brush into it. Don't overload the brush with paint. Apply the paint in a tapping motion holding the brush straight up and down. Let each letter dry before doing the next so that it won't smear under the stencil sheet. When this dries turn the cube over and do the opposite side the same way.

Set the rack inside the cube, fill it with wine, and put it on display.

# flowered fabric dresser

Cut-out paper designs have always been associated with decoupage. Fabric has rarely been used in this kind of crafting. While the process is similar it is actually much easier.

The emphasis in decoupage is on cutting and with fabric this step is not at all exacting. As a matter of fact, the cutting for this project is very loose, as you can see from the close-up photograph. Of course the color of the furniture must be the same as the background color of the fabric. For instance, this dresser is painted white because the fabric in back of the flowers is white. In this way the flowers appear to be perfectly cut out, while in fact much of the excess fabric is left around and between the flowers, stems, and leaves.

When selecting fabric choose a design that will look well on the object and that will not be too difficult to cut. The weight is another consideration. If the material is very fragile it is more likely to fray and create a ragged edge when cut than a heavy fabric might. For this purpose I used a "Scotchgard" mill-treated Waverly material. To extend the design idea, you could use the same material for pillows, curtains, a bedspread or even wallcovering. (To apply the fabric to the walls use a fabric adhesive.) If the fabric has not been treated you can do this yourself by spraying it with Scotchgard. This will protect the fabric from soil and will stiffen it for easy cutting and handling.

If you buy extra fabric it can be used to line the drawers as well. This is a nice finishing touch.

The materials needed for this project are: a three-drawer wooden dresser; printed fabric (Waverly Royal Copenhagen here); Spra-Ment adhesive; Krylon clear spray varnish; white latex wall paint; a drop of brown acrylic paint; cuticle and straight scissors; sandpaper; a 2-inch paint brush; 6 small, round porcelain knobs.

Prepare the dresser by sanding it smooth and wiping away traces of sand dust. Remove the drawers and give all exposed wood a prime coat of latex paint. When this dries sand the furniture lightly to remove any bumps or particles that have dried in the paint. Apply a second coat of paint to the front of the drawers. When this dries, another coat may be necessary. The drawers should be smooth and well coated. Since the paint takes only a few minutes to dry it is best to give them as many coats as needed.

Pour some of the latex paint into a jar and mix a drop of brown acrylic paint into it. This should be done sparingly. Put a drop in at a time, mix well, then test the color on a separate piece of wood. What you are trying to achieve is a very subtle beige for the contrasting top and sides of the bureau. Remember that a large area always appears darker in color than a

Carefully cut flowers from the fabric.

It is difficult to cut fabric as neatly as paper designs.

Spray backs of flowers with Spra-Ment adhesive.

small patch, so stay on the light side when mixing. A drop of the color is quite intense.

Paint the top and sides. Be sure to mix enough of the color to give the dresser two coats if necessary. It is difficult to mix the exact color twice, therefore have enough to begin with. When this is dry the painted surface should be sanded lightly.

With the straight scissors, cut out each square from the fabric. The more delicate cutting should be done with the cuticle scissors; they're difficult to use on fabric, so reserve them for tiny, hard-to-get-at areas. Do not cut too close to weak areas, such as around stems, or the flower will break apart. Cutting should not take long. I cut all the flowers for this dresser in an evening of television-watching, or rather, listening.

Arrange the cut-out flowers on the drawers. Work with one drawer at a time. Keep arranging and rearranging until the design is the way you think it looks best. Sometimes one flower may appear to be too heavy when placed next to more

Firmly roll over each flower as it is placed on the dresser.

fragile ones. A leaf or petal can be cut or added where necessary. In other words, adjust the designs to please yourself. Save a bud or leaf to place around one of the knobs. I find it easiest to put all the drawers on a work area where I can see the relationship between them as I arrange the designs.

When the flowers look well they can be prepared for permanent placement. Taking one at a time, turn each flower over on a piece of scrap cardboard and spray the back with adhesive. Lift it carefully and place it on the drawer front. Press it down with the palm of your hand. If you have a roller (a rolling pin will do, but a rubber brayer is best), run it over the flower to secure it to the surface. Be sure all edges are glued down firmly. If the fabric lifts around the edges, remove the flower and spray it again.

When all the flowers have been placed on the drawers check each one to be sure it is secure. Next spray each drawer with the varnish. This should be done with fine, even strokes to avoid any dripping or accumulation of varnish in an area.

Give the rest of the bureau an even coating of varnish. Let it dry about twenty minutes before coating again. To best protect the paint and fabric, at least five coats of varnish should be applied. This will give your piece a tough protective coating and the designs will be permanently affixed.

These bureaus come with standard wooden or metal knobs, but they seemed too heavy for this design. I found small, round porcelain knobs. They're delicate and do not detract from the design. Hardware stores are a good source of variety knobs; you might find others that work as well.

If you line the drawers with fabric, precut each side and bottom so that each piece is a little bit larger than the drawers. In this way the inside edges can all overlap slightly so that no wood cracks show. Apply the fabric with the spray adhesive as you did the cut-out flowers. The fabric used here was already mill-treated and did not need additional protection. If your fabric is not treated, spray a coating of varnish inside the drawers, and you're finished.

# fanciful stool and storage cube

# fanciful stool and storage cube

This small wooden stool combines various coloring materials to create a bright, bold motif. It may look as though you must have some artistic talent, or at least a basic knowledge of painting, but this is the best part of the project: *Anyone* can do it and not mess it up. There is absolutely no way that this project will not turn out well. You can do anything with the colors and the designs and it's a lot of fun because of this.

We've provided the design used here, but your own ideas can come from anywhere. Simple designs work best since, as you can see, no fine details are used. The basic technique is that of applying felt tip marker, watercolor dyes, oil crayons and shellac over one another. Each time a different element is introduced the colors change—and this is why you can't go wrong. If you don't like the way the design looks, a color can be removed, changed or emphasized. Since the design has a primitive look the project should, in no way, be intimidating to do.

The flat surface of a stool is perfect for this project as it is easy to work on and is small enough so that the entire top can be filled with the design. It's also rather neat to sit on when finished. I'm still convinced that I will walk away with a reverse imprint of an alligator on the seat of my pants. But the design is permanent even though it looks as though it could be rubbed off easily—another one of its charms.

The materials you need are: a small wooden stool; a 16-inch cube; tracing paper; a pencil; oil crayons; a black felt-tip, water-soluble marker; watercolor dyes; shellac and denatured alcohol; a brush; sandpaper; two or three small artist's brushes.

Most crafts products have substitutes. However, this is one time when a substitute for any of the materials used will cause a disaster. The project simply will not work. For example, many people think that shellac is the same as varnish. It isn't. Shellac dissolves in alcohol, varnish in turpentine or mineral spirits. If varnish is used in place of shellac it will cause the design to smear.

Sand the stool smooth. Rule a 1-inch grid and scale the design up to size. Rub black pencil over the back of the design. Tape the tracing to the top of the stool. Using a ball-point pen, go over the entire outline while pressing down firmly. Remove the tracing and the outline will be transferred to the stool top. There will be a double outline around the design. This area is colored in with the felt-tip marker. Your design will be accented with a thick black outline. This does not have to be absolutely precise and is probably what I like best about this crafting technique.

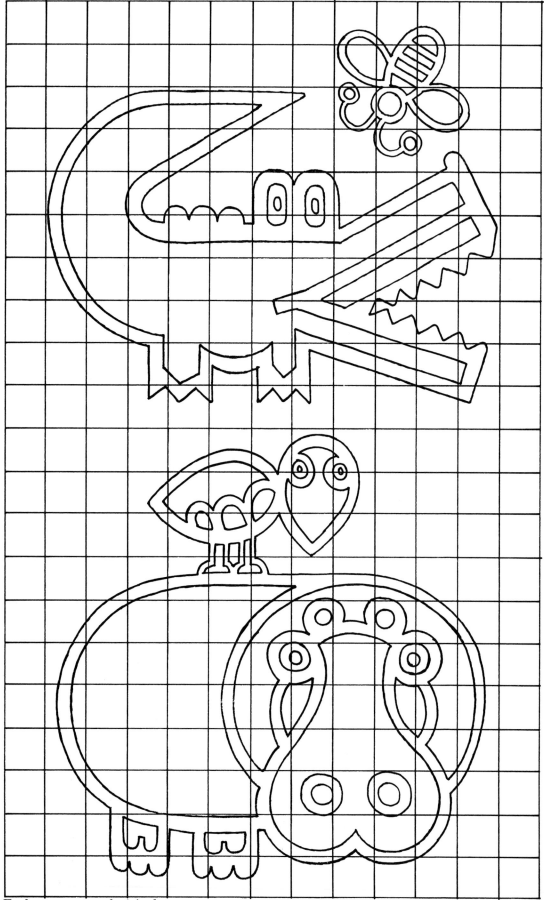

Each square equals 1 inch.

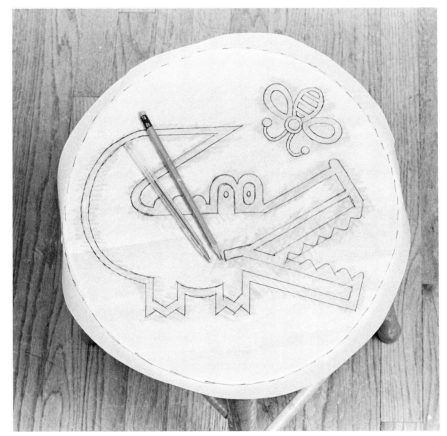
Transfer tracing to stool top.

Next use the watercolor dyes to begin to fill in the design. Watercolor dyes are not the same as colored India ink. They are available in art supply stores. The brand used here is Luma. Using a small, flat watercolor brush, first paint the alligator with bright green dye. Stay inside the black line as the black marker doesn't mix well with the dye. Wash out the brush before applying the next color. Test each color on a piece of wood before using; they sometimes come out much differently than they appear in the bottle. Since the dyes are transparent the wood background shows through and darkens the colors. If you want a lighter color, put a bit in a small glass and dilute it with a little water. You can also mix dyes to create any color you want.

Paint the top half of the stool around the alligator with yellow or orange, the bottom portion with raspberry or rose tyren. The bumblebee's wings are blue and the body orange.

Outline design with thick black marker.

Fill in design using watercolor dyes.

Add color with oil crayons.

When the dyes have been used to fill in the entire design, continue the fanciful colors with oil crayons. These add brightness and detail. It is a good idea to buy a set of oil crayons with a variety of colors to choose from. Our set cost three dollars.

Fill in the wings with a bright blue and make alligator scales with a bright shocking green. Add yellow to the bee's back and pale rose around the alligator's eyes. The squiggly lines simulating waves are a lighter pink. If you find you don't like a color after it has been applied, simply rub another over it. You can do almost anything you want with this technique.

To tone down some of the colors, rub over them with another color. The orange was made lighter by rubbing over it with peach. When you have achieved a pleasing effect, go over the outline with a black oil crayon to darken it.

Brush a coating of shellac over the design and let this dry. The colors will become very bright and shiny and take on a glazed appearance. When this dries add more color where

Coat design with shellac for a bright, shiny permanent finish.

desired with the oil crayons. The total effect should be bright, fanciful, almost batik-like. Shellac again and let it dry. If more color is needed, continue this process until you're satisfied. You can stop anywhere along the way. There is no way to make a mistake.

A variation on this technique can be used for a different look. First draw in the black outline, then route it out with a Dremel Moto tool, a high speed drill with a round head. (We tried using a regular drill, but it didn't work; you need the speed of the Dremel tool.) The outline can then be filled in with burnt sienna watercolor dye for an added dimension. Continue as before.

Coat the final design with shellac for a shiny permanent finish. If you want to continue down the legs, you can add color in the same way. For an added touch you might like to follow this process with a design that could be traced onto a wooden wall plaque.

*150*

# comic book table

# comic book table

Covering a table with comic book covers and pages is an inexpensive, off-beat idea, appropriate for a child's room or even a family room. The pastel colors overlap and blend together for interesting coloration. Once you get going on this project it is easy to do, but there are some tricky points to know before you begin. The paper is very thin and the ink is poor, therefore you have to use the correct materials and avoid shortcuts or you will have a mess. The printed paper is pretty awful.

Besides the colors, the texture is interesting. While all the papers overlap, the varnished finish gives the table an overall smooth feel. It's fun to read the comics right through the varnish.

Collect a batch of different comic books as well as newspaper strips. You can use black and white, but the colored funnies are prettier. You need a lot of them, so get your kids' friends to do some donating. I found that it wasn't easy to find comic books everywhere, so if you find a place that sells them get as many as you think you'll need. I can't say for sure how many were used for this as I just kept cutting them up as they were acquired and lost count. A good variety was used, so more books were needed than if they had all come from the same source. No violent strips, only Archie and Jughead and friends decorate this particular table. But of course, the subject matter is up to you.

A nice aspect of this project is the lack of planned design. The pieces are simply cut up (not ripped) and slapped here and there until all surfaces are covered. This project could also be done using a cube to make a comic book container, a toy chest, or a night table for insomniac reading.

The materials used should be exactly as recommended. After some experimentation I found that these materials are the only ones that work: an 18-inch parson's table; sandpaper; glossy polymer medium (made by Grumbacher, Weber, Liquitex and others); a sponge brush; scissors; a selection of comic books; a sponge; a rubber brayer (optional); glossy, clear,

Apply comic-book strips at random over table top.

polyurethane; a 2-inch paint brush; paint thinner; 0000 steel wool; wax.

The polyurethane gives the table a final, tough protective coating. The polymer medium can be used as an undercoat and as a final coat, but it will not be durable enough as a table top finish. If you are making a storage cube or toy box you could eliminate buying the polyurethane, 2-inch brush and paint thinner, unless you need them for other projects. A small can is also useful.

Cut up strips of comic book pages. The covers can also be

used. Turn all the comics face down on a work surface. This could be the kitchen counter—do not use newspaper. Using the sponge applicator coat the back of all the paper with polymer medium. It will go on milky white, but will dry clear. It will wash off the counter top if sponged up before it dries. Let the coated comic strips dry. This will only take minutes. Turn all the pieces over, coat the front and let them dry.

Next, apply the polymer medium to a section of the table. Do only a small area since it dries quickly and you need to work while it's very wet. Place one of the comic strips on the wet surface and press it down. Coat it lightly with the medium; if foam forms on the paper it will not dry clear. Continue to cover the table in this way. Overlap all the edges and corners as you proceed to make a collage. Extend the design over the edges of the table and down the legs. They can be placed at random—sideways, upside down, it doesn't matter. As you do this the colors will merge and blend in a very subtle way. When you are finished rinse your brush out well in water. Sponge brushes are meant for one-time use, but if cleaned well can be used again.

Right here I would like to state a warning. If you use an oil base varnish instead of the polymer medium the print will smear and run together. Also, the picture from one side will show through the other side making all the words and pictures totally illegible. Once both sides have a coating of the medium applied to them they are sealed and regular varnish can be applied on top. The polymer medium is used as a gluing agent in this case as well as a sealer for the comics.

Coat all surfaces with glossy polyurethane. This is an oil base plastic resin and will give the table a hard, protective finish. It takes twenty-four hours to dry and must be painted on evenly in one direction. Start at the center of the table and work toward the outer edges to prevent what is known as "roll over," the collection of excess varnish at the edges which dries in a hard ridge. When coating the legs apply a thin layer of polyurethane. Two or three coats are best, letting each dry thoroughly before adding another.

Finally, rub the entire piece with very fine steel wool and apply a coat of furniture paste wax. If you have chosen to eliminate the polyurethane the piece will need several coats of polymer medium to give it a final finish. This dries within ten or fifteen minutes, therefore the project can be completed in one day. The finish will not be as smooth as the polyurethane, however, and will turn white if anything wet (such as a glass) is left on it. Other than these drawbacks, the finish is extremely tough.

# fabric-covered table

# fabric-covered table

A large parson's table can be used as a desk or as a dining table. It is also narrow enough to be used in a hallway or as a dining room sideboard. If you are covering a table with fabric it should be heavy, soil-resistant material, preferably in dark colors. The fabric used here is canvas and the background is black. The bold stripes are very bright red, yellow and green. This project takes a bit of precision and if you are basically careless, it will try your patience. However, it is not difficult and the results are rewarding.

This is the only project in the book that I actually did twice. Fortunately, I had enough fabric. I am not usually that patient and ordinarily would have given up, but I liked the idea and thought it was good to have one failure for the experience. Besides, if I hadn't redone the whole thing I wouldn't have known if it would work. My basic curiosity got the better of me.

The project as planned was to cover the table with the fabric, adding stripes as a runner on top and in bands around the top and bottom of the legs. Once covered, the table was to have a coating of varnish to make it smooth, shiny and hard. Unfortunately, the varnish did not float over the surface of the fabric the way it does with wood. It completely penetrated the fabric, reacted negatively with the fabric adhesive underneath, and created a mess. Nine times out of ten luck, combined with experience, is on my side. It took a long time to cover the table, matching the stripes and hiding seam

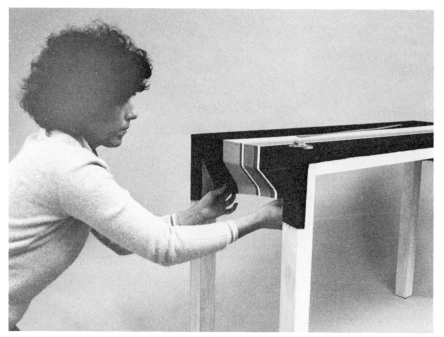

Stretch fabric down and under the edge of the table.

edges. It took approximately five minutes to ruin the entire thing. I did it over—removed the fabric and covered the table again!

Now I am very careful to make tests when using new techniques or products. So, to be sure, the instructions for doing this project have been thoroughly tested.

Materials needed are: 18 by 48 by 30-inch parson's table; 3 yards of fabric; Spra-Ment fabric adhesive; a razor blade; a metal ruler; Scotchgard fabric protector.

Measure and cut a long piece of fabric for the top. It should be large enough to cover the front edge of all sides. Spread the fabric face down on newspaper and spray the back liberally with Spra-Ment adhesive. Press one end of the sticky fabric to the side of the table so that there is enough fabric to tuck under the edge. From the other end of the table pull the fabric taut and gently lay it across the table. If the fabric is striped, take extra care to make sure the stripes lie straight. Smooth the fabric over the table with your hand. If you have a wallpaper brush it will come in handy here. Be sure to smooth away any air bubbles that may be trapped under the fabric. If you don't get the fabric down right the first time, simply lift it off and lay it down again. Press the sides and tuck the fabric securely under the table. This can later be stapled to the underside if necessary.

Next, measure and cut the pieces for the legs. If it is possible, cut one continuous piece for each leg so that they

Apply leg pieces so that seams do not show.

can be wrapped with only one seam. Plan this so that the end pieces of material join to form a seam on the leg where it won't show. If the table will be against a wall then all seams can be toward the back where they will not be seen.

Spray each piece of fabric as it is used and wrap each leg carefully. Tuck the end of the piece under so that it glues to itself. Spray some Spra-Ment on the back side of the leg and adjust the fabric so that the back seam runs straight up and down at the edge. The fabric should fit as tightly as possible. With a blade, cut off any excess at the bottom of each leg for a neat finish.

In order to get the effect shown here I had to piece the fabric on the legs. Since everyone can't get the exact same fabric you may have different problems to deal with depending on the material used. This particular fabric has stripes running down the center. In order to carry the same theme onto the legs it was necessary to cut pieces for the top and bottom of the legs. Since the background is black it wasn't difficult to hide the seam where these pieces come together; I simply overlapped the two. If you are going to be doing something a little bit out-of-the-ordinary with the fabric you choose, buy enough for error and for piecing when you can't cut the fabric in the most economical way.

To protect the fabric from soiling, apply two or three coats of Scotchgard fabric protector. Spray the entire surface, let it dry and reapply. Stay away from varnish.

# child's block table

A friend of mine has an old-fashioned country store that is chock-full of antiques and handmade items. The objects are always different as the store is small and the business brisk. She is especially fond of old-fashioned children's games and toys and one day, while browsing, I came upon a sand pail filled with old playing blocks. With unfinished cubes still on my mind one connected with the other and I realized that a giant block would make a great table for a child's room. "Take the blocks," Sharon offered. "My contribution to the book." And so another design idea was cemented.

The blocks for the top of the cube are not so unusual and came from a local toy store. While this project is attractive in a small child's room it actually serves three purposes. First of all, when the blocks are filled on the recessed top the cube can be used as a table. Next, the blocks can be rearranged so that they spell out words making this an educational game table. Finally, it is a perfect way to keep a child's blocks neat and out of the way.

Again the cube with a recessed top (or back or bottom) is used. We have included the design for this project, but you might find an old block that has a nice design that you might adapt. As you can see, this project is easy enough for a young person to do.

Robin Brunhuber painting surface with white latex paint.

The materials needed are: a 16-inch cube with one recessed side (from J. C. Penney); 18 by 20-inch sheets of tracing paper; ¾-inch masking tape; white latex paint; red, blue, green and orange spray paint; rubber cement; an X-acto knife; and 121 children's letter blocks (Playskool 1 ⁵/₁₆-inch blocks fit).

Prepare the cube by sanding and filling in any depressed areas with wood filler. When this dries, sand, and paint the cube with white paint. If you use one-coat interior latex paint, the cube will look best with two coats. I know this sounds contradictory, but while it is called one-coat, the fact is that two coats are almost always needed, especially when using white.

Each square equals 2 inches.

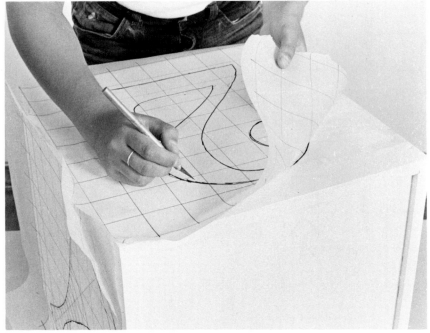
Cut design out with X-acto knife and remove excess paper.

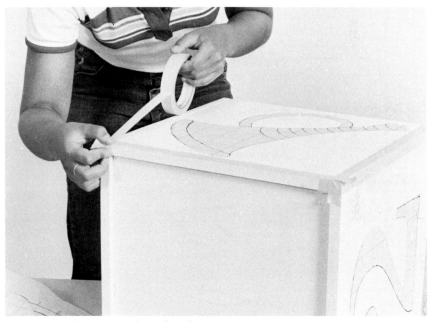
Mask off edges to make a border.

Make a grid and scale up the designs on the tracing paper. Coat the back of the tracing paper design and the side of the cube with rubber cement. Let both surfaces dry. Mount the design in position using a tracing paper slipsheet. The slipsheet is another sheet of tracing paper that goes between the two cemented surfaces until you get the design positioned just right and tack down one edge. Then you can remove the slipsheet a little at a time, smoothing down the paper design as you go.

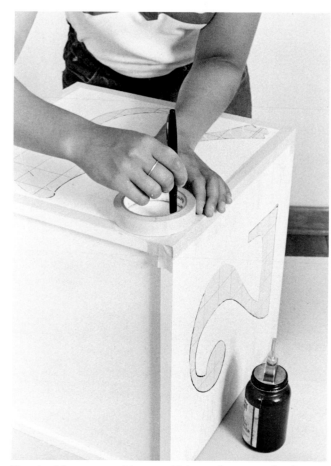
Use inside curve of tape roll to make curved edges.

Spray bright-colored paint on each side of cube.

When the tracing paper designs are securely mounted on all sides, cut each one out with an X-acto knife and peel away extra paper around the design. You're now left with an area to be filled in. Rub off the rubber cement residue with your finger or a rubber cement pick-up.

To make the border at the edge of the cube, run strips of ¾-inch masking tape along each edge. Then fill in the corners with a few more strips of tape. Using the inside curve of the roll of masking tape, draw a curved line joining the straight strips of tape. Cut through this curved line with the X-acto knife and remove the excess tape. This will leave you with a

Remove paper with aid of knife blade.

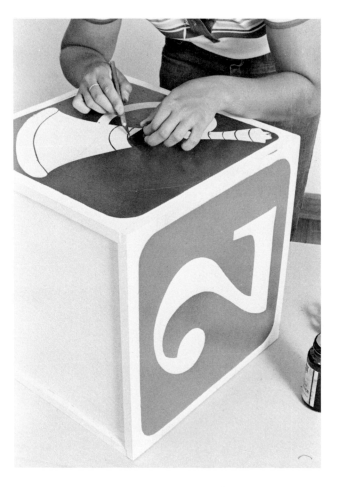

rounded corner. With all the designs in place and all the edges taped and rounded you are ready to paint. Bright colors, such as those used here, will cover in one coat. Spray the color on evenly. Go back and forth as you spray until the side is completely covered. The paint will dry very quickly.

Remove the paper very carefully with the aid of the knife blade at the edges. Pull the tape off; the edges will lift easily.

The blocks that fit in the top of the cube are meant to be movable so that different words can be spelled out or games developed. Playskool makes letter blocks that fit comfortably; 121 of these blocks fill the area.

# tulip-covered table

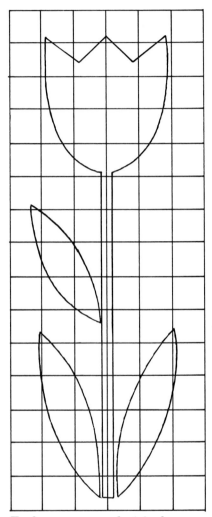

Each square equals 1 inch.

The tulip design for an outdoor table makes use of the variety of colors that can be found in construction paper. The placement of the tulips surrounding the table makes them appear to be growing up from the ground.

The materials needed for this project are: one 16-inch cube; sandpaper; wood filler if needed; white latex paint; 1-inch paint brush; a variety package of construction paper; scissors; a pencil; Elmer's glue; glossy polyurethane varnish; brush cleaner.

Begin by sanding and painting the surface of the cube. When the paint dries, reapply before sanding the surface smooth again. Clean the brush in water so that it can be used again. Next, trace and scale the diagram to size. Each square of the grid is equal to 1 inch. Turn the tracing over and transfer the tulip design onto the construction paper. You will need three tulips in each color. This table is made up of orange, green, blue and yellow flowers. The shorter tulips are created by cutting down the stems and removing a leaf.

Spread the back of each paper element with glue and press it in place on the side of the cube. When all sides are covered trace and cut out four tulip heads to be used for the top. Each will match the color of its corresponding side. Repeat this procedure for the corner trim. Glue these in place on the top of the table.

Apply a coat of glossy polyurethane varnish to all exposed areas. Let this dry overnight before applying another coat for extra protection. Soak the varnish brush in paint cleaner. After two or three varnish applications the brush can be thrown away.

# ceramic tile table

Another parson's table! I don't think there is ever an end to the creative ideas that can be adapted for the basic shape of a parson's table. My preference has always been the 18-inch square. Not only is it a comfortable size to design for, but it is a versatile size and shape for many uses. The wood takes stain or paint well and no matter how complicated the craft, the object is small enough to do a good job with little time invested. The raw wood of most parson's tables is usually smooth and light and quite handsome as is. A coat of satin varnish will bring out the natural beauty of the wood while giving it a lustrous protective finish.

This table is stained with Minwax walnut stain for a deep rich brown. The tiles used for the top are inexpensive 4¼-inch bathroom tiles, available in flooring supply stores. The stark, white tiles on the darkly stained wood contrast sharply for a dramatic effect. However, tiles come in a variety of colors. Choose the color that suits you best, but be sure it will serve as a pleasing background for the painted design.

The floral design on the tiles is adapted from one of the plates in Dover Publications' *A Treasury of Design for Artists and Craftsmen*. Books like this are good sources of ideas. Any design can be scaled to size and transferred to the tiles, but the Art Nouveau design used here seemed to be made for this table. The paints are permanent once applied, so the tiles do not have to be fired. They can be wiped when dirty and the color will remain.

The materials needed are: an 18-inch parson's table; an 8-foot length of ¼-inch quarter round molding; a miter box and saw; ¾-inch brads; eighteen 4¼-inch glossy white ceramic tiles; a variety of enamel craft paint colors (Talen's and Testor's are available in hobby shops); paint thinner and medium; small- and medium-sized natural hair brushes; a sheet of 18 by 24-inch tracing paper; Minwax walnut stain; a sponge brush; indoor wood varnish; sandpaper; tile cement; putty knife.

There are two different aspects to this project: preparing the table and creating the design on the tiles.

Begin by sanding the table and wiping away any sand dust. Mix the stain and apply it to the table with the sponge brush applicator. This is an inexpensive two-inch brush that looks like a sponge on the end of a stick. I find this works best for staining and many paint jobs, however some people prefer to rub stain on with a cloth. Coat the legs and sides and the top rim of the table with the stain. Let this sink in for fifteen minutes. It will seal the wood as it penetrates. Wipe away the excess by rubbing the entire surface with a cloth. Since the Minwax is an oil base stain it will take a full day to dry. Stain the strip of molding in the same way. This should be done before the molding is attached to the table.

The molding serves both to hold the tiles in position and to finish off the edges. A cross section view of quarter round

Each square equals 1 inch.

molding looks like a quarter of a circle. Sitting on the edge of the table, it makes a small rounded edge where the tiles meet the edge of the table. Quarter-inch molding on each edge will take up a half inch of the 18-inch table. Four tiles 4½-inch square should take up the 17 inches that are left, but they don't! They actually fill a 17¾-inch space. The bumps on the edges of the tiles must be ground down slightly so that they butt together. A sharpening stone is used for this.

The corners of the molding must be mitered so that they fit correctly and look well. A miter box is an inexpensive item that you use to slide the molding into. It has slots for a saw to fit into, making it possible to cut an exact 45-degree angle. A miter box costs less than three dollars and can be useful for making picture frames as well.

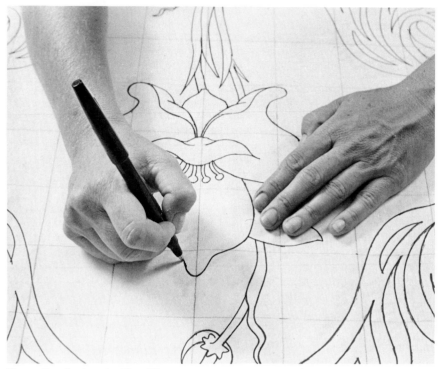
Transfer design to the tiles.

Once cut, attach the molding with Elmer's glue to the top edges of the table. Secure the molding with ¾-inch brads. The molding should come to the very edge of the table and butt at the corners. Wipe away any excess glue that has oozed out of the edges.

The walnut stain will appear flat and dull when dry. To bring out the luster and give the wood a beautiful finish, apply a coat of satin indoor wood varnish. The sponge applicator cleaned with paint thinner can be used to do this. However, since these brushes are so inexpensive (approximately thirty-five to fifty cents) it might be a good idea to buy one for staining and another for varnishing. Coat the stained areas and allow the varnish to dry overnight. Another coat or two is recommended, but not absolutely necessary.

Next make a grid of 2-inch squares and blow up the design to fit the table top. This is done on the large sheet of tracing paper using the grid method described earlier. Rub pencil over the back of the outline of the design. Place the tiles on a work surface and line them up so that they are as even as possible. Lay the tracing paper design over the tiles and tape the paper to the work surface. Go over the outline with a ballpoint pen making sure not to move the tiles underneath. The pencil marks on the reverse side will transfer the design to the tiles.

A variety of enamel craft paint colors are applied with artist's brush.

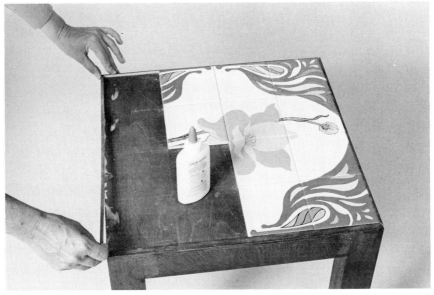

Table edging is made of quarter-round molding.

Remove the tracing and you will have a faint pencil outline of the design to be filled in. Outline the design with black permanent felt-tip pen. This Art Nouveau design looks best in soft, delicate colors reminiscent of this style. Hobby paints are used here, small inexpensive bottles of paint meant for painting model planes and boats. There are many colors to choose from and further shades can be mixed, even if you have different brands.

Small artist's brushes made of natural hair are best for this job. They are soft and pointed and if you have two or three different sizes you won't have difficulty painting any of the areas. When the paint dries it will be permanent.

To affix the tiles to the table top use tile cement. It can be purchased in a hardware store; a small can is plenty. Spread the cement over the top of the table with a small putty knife. Set the tiles in place so that they fit together tightly. Let the cement dry before using the table.

# on your own

When the last project was completed we were just getting revved up. Suddenly I had the urge to do many more projects that we hadn't thought of before. Obviously, we didn't and couldn't do everything there is to do with unfinished furniture. Large pieces such as china cabinets, storage beds, wall units, bookcases, desks, and many more were some of the items left undone. However, many of the design ideas that we did carry out were intended as just that—ideas. The item was not always the important thing. The design could be executed on a variety of furniture pieces. We chose what we felt our readers could and would do. The book is meant for inspiration.

As we came upon obstacles we tried to work out simple solutions so that the novice could do each project with ease. I hope we have achieved our goal: to give you some creative inspiration for achieving professional-looking results without spending a fortune or investing too much time. The materials that were used are readily available. Nothing angers me more than to read about an intriguing project only to find that something is missing—the instructions aren't complete or the craftworker has used a hard-to-find material. Or worse yet, the writer doesn't say what the material is. I have tried to avoid any of these errors so that you can successfully, and enjoyably, complete any of these projects.

## the little boxes

While working on each project there was always a stage where paint or varnish was drying. During these waiting periods I began to make miniature designs on small boxes that I had. Each of the bureaus has a box to go with it. The patchwork chest has a matching wastebasket. Look for the rounded box on the coffee table and the suede-covered box with the parson's table. They are commonly found in craft shops. In case you missed seeing them in the photos while working on the furniture projects, you might like to go back and consider these as well. If you aren't sure about a crafting technique this is a good way to try your hand before plunging into the furniture project. They make easy but delightful gifts and are certainly an added detail for placing on top of the furniture. Each one is done exactly as the technique is described; however, you will have to work out your own dimensions according to the box size. Mine were made with leftover scraps.